LORD JESUS CHRIST, master carpenter of Nazareth, who through the cross of wood and nails has wrought mans full SALVATION: wield well your tools in this your workshop that we who come TO YOU rough hewn may be FASHIONED to a truer and fuller BEAUTY in your name and for your GLORY. amen.

To Andrew & Cleone with love & best wishes — and with thanks for all your support and encouragement

Peter

AN APPRENTICE IN THE
LORD'S WORKSHOP

THE ESTABLISHMENT OF LETTON HALL AS A CHRISTIAN CENTRE

PETER CARROLL

ALDERWAY BOOKS
www.alderway.com

Published by
Alderway Books, Norwich, England.
www.alderway.com

Unless otherwise indicated, biblical quotations are taken from the New International Version (NIV) © 1973, 1978, 1984 by the International Bible Society.

ISBN 978-1-908667-38-0

Cover design by MPH.

The cover image is of a carving by Steve Eggleton and is used with kind permission. Photo taken by Peter Carroll.

To my lovely, supportive, and long-suffering family.

CONTENTS

(Contents overleaf)

APPENDICES CONTENTS

FOREWORD

Peter Carroll's use of the metaphor 'workshop,' as found in the prayer that is skilfully carved out of the great single section of ancient oak in the library at Letton Hall, exactly catches the challenges and lessons of realizing the vision of Letton Hall as a 'House for the Lord.'

Peter, although conveying to us the hopes and trials, the many, many people involved, and the amazing and surprising ways God has rewarded almost daring faith, omits perhaps one of the most abiding and greatest encouragements anyone involved with Letton Hall will have encountered. He fails here simply because of who he is. When he asked me to write a foreword I felt I could never do justice to the task but there was one thought that immediately sprang to mind and that was the thought of the kind of man Peter is. I hinted that I would need to say something about him and he immediately fired back, "Perhaps I have asked the wrong person!" Typically modest, quick witted and cheerful.

Peter has been a magnet for the many helpers, volunteers and workers. He could not have explained in his account of his 'apprenticeship in the workshop' the qualities that made him the key under God to so much of the success of the whole enterprise. He is one of the greatest examples of a Christian I have known. He genuinely seems to like everybody and brings an easy charm and affability together with a pioneering spirit and visionary daring - all with a sincere faith and true love of God.

On some occasions I have been humbled and truly blessed when I have seen fellow trustees or helpers tell him what he can or cannot do in the house he actually owned, only to see him smile and graciously consider what seemed like an impudence, though genuinely meant to help find God's way. He has been a wonderful example to all who worked with him and shed much light and sprinkled not a little salt on quite a few difficult situations. God be praised! In many ways, Letton Hall is not only

'A house for the Lord' but the house of God's man. All who enjoyed working with him through seemingly impossible situations to fulfil the vision for the glory of God give thanks to God for him.

His history of the work at Letton Hall teaches us many lessons in Christian guidance and faith. Letton Hall has seen great excitement and encouragements, some severe trials and tests of faith, many wonderful friendships and hundreds of people blessed by God. Not the least of the means of blessing have been the different teams of workers and helpers, as well as the guests and visitors, but especially Peter Carroll and his family, for which I thank God here personally and also on behalf of the many others who have played any part in the 'Workshop' that is Letton Hall.

E. Gwyn Jordan

ABOUT THIS BOOK

This book is very much *my* book. Not that it is *about* me; rather, it is about the work of God in establishing Letton Hall in the heart of rural Norfolk as a Christian Centre; but it is written from my point of view. Many people have been involved in this team project over the last thirty-five years and many have told me their stories or reminded me of events and occasions, but I have felt able to write only from my own direct experience. So, although I am very grateful for their valuable input, all the mistakes and omissions are mine.

I have included only the very minimum of names of people, in order to preserve a sense of narrative in what I have written. However, as the project progressed over the years, issues of "Letton News" were sent out, including all the latest developments, as a stage-by-stage story, with full details of everyone involved. It has been tempting to include all of these as an appendix to this book, but such was the level of activity and so great was the number of people on these "rolls of honour," that the appendices would have dwarfed the book several times over(!) Instead, I have included various extracts and reproduced one issue of Letton News in full (Appendix 23, p.193). The full series of more than fifty issues is available at Letton Hall.

This is the Lord's story and may it be to His glory. I have felt compelled to write it as I am in a unique position, having been in from the start. I have a real sense of the Holy Spirit being at work and hope that what I have written may be a reminder of that work and an encouragement to others who may be living out similar experiences.

Peter Carroll

CHAPTER ONE

APPRENTICE TO THE LORD

There is a carved oak plaque above the fireplace in the Library at Letton Hall setting out a prayer:

Lord Jesus Christ, Master Carpenter of Nazareth,
who through the cross of wood and nails has wrought
man's full salvation,
Wield well your tools in this your workshop
that we who come to you rough hewn may be fashioned
to a truer and fuller beauty,
in your name and for your glory. Amen

I've always liked the thought of Letton Hall being a *workshop* – a place where people can come and stay for a day or a week or even longer, and experience God at work in practical and tangible ways.

In the twenty-five years I spent living and working there, from being deeply involved in establishing it until the time I retired from active involvement at sixty-five, I have felt very much like an apprentice to the Lord (albeit a mature one), in the Lord's workshop.

An apprentice is someone who is 'bound' – committed, indentured – to learn from a skilled person, for a period of time, and works for low wages. There is a feeling of being a beginner at something – a rookie.

Plaque above the fireplace in the Letton Hall Library. Carved by Steve Eggleton; this picture used by kind permission.

I had learnt something of this process long before arriving at Letton. Having graduated from university with an honours degree in Engineering Science, it wasn't until I became a Graduate Apprentice immediately afterwards that I began to realise what engineering was really all about – even to the point of knowing which bit was the nut and which the bolt! There were many similarities between my engineering apprenticeship and my apprenticeship to the Lord.

There was a lot of learning to be done in both apprenticeships just by watching – seeing the Lord produce miracles out of otherwise hopeless situations; watching him work in people's lives, transforming them. There were also times when nothing seemed to be happening, and when sitting around watching became quite tedious – just as in my engineering apprenticeship, I had sometimes to learn by the seemingly boring process of "sitting beside Nelly." Often, it was not until long afterwards that I realised how much I had absorbed.

More exciting moments come in an apprenticeship when we are allowed to do the work ourselves. "Try it," our patient instructor says, "I leave it to you." And having learnt how to use the tools and resources we have available, we can experience the thrill of producing results, often with our teacher looking quietly over our shoulder with shared pride.

An apprenticeship is not a well-paid job! Later chapters of Letton Hall's history document the perpetual struggle to make ends meet – but the aim is survival rather than surfeit. Apprentices often have to carry out menial tasks that others could be paid to do and to work long hours, all in order to keep down costs, but this is part of the commitment required by being indentured. It is a consideration that has to be faced by all those who see the attractions of Christian service and say, "Send me."

There is real fellowship in the workshop. Fellow apprentices arrive from different backgrounds and with different skills and abilities, and all work side-by-side, learning from each other and from the Lord.

Apprenticeships vary in length, maybe from only a week or so, up to many years, and people may leave to take up work in other 'workshops'. In my case, it lasted for a major part of my working life, from around forty years old, with both an engineering and a management career already behind me. It is interesting that the Lord often uses our previous experience as we embark on an apprenticeship with him ...

But the first step for me as an apprentice to the Lord was to find the workshop.

CHAPTER TWO

LOCATING THE WORKSHOP

The story began in 1978. I was a controlling director of our small-to-medium-size family owned business (turnover around £10m in today's values), and after ten years of growth and development, I was thinking hard about the way ahead.

We had started out as importing agents for North-American-made metal bits and pieces for the building and retail hardware world and had diversified into some manufacturing ourselves, and even some exporting – and there were several options to consider: consolidate or diversify further? Manufacture more or buy in more? Import more or export more?

Somehow, I couldn't see a five-year business plan that seemed right. In fact, I couldn't even see a six-month plan that I felt would appeal to and challenge our lively and enthusiastic company team. As a Christian in business, prayer was one of my management tools, and as the future seemed less and less clear, and the closer it got, so my prayer got more and more urgent.

I would be asked by my team "Which way are we going Peter?" To which my reply usually was, "I'm thinking ..."

"Well hurry up," was the rejoinder from at least one of my managers. "While *you're* thinking *we* might be sinking!"

And as my prayer became more desperate, so I got up earlier and earlier each day to pray, sitting in my familiar prayer chair (which I still have), reading the bible and laying everything before the Lord.

On Thursday 17th August 1978 at around 7.15 in the morning, as the note in the front of my bible reminds me, I was reading 1 Thessalonians, verses 11 and 12 of chapter 4:

> *This should be your ambition; to live a quiet life, minding your own business and doing your own work, just as we told you before. As a result, people who are not Christians will trust and respect you, and you will not need to depend on others for enough money to pay your bills.* **1 Thessalonians 4:11-12, The Living Bible**

Actually, this was not the translation I was reading at the time, but the Living Bible sets out the meaning that leapt out at me that morning. It's not much of a specific business plan, reading it afresh now, especially the bit about "leading a quiet life," but somehow a full and detailed management programme flashed into my mind – and it was just right for the situation.

As I took a cup of tea up to my wife Mary, she took one look at me and said, "You look as if you've seen a vision!" And when a wife who's known you for more than twenty years says that, it confirms that certainly something significant has happened. You had better pay attention!

By noon that morning, the company was transformed. It was mainly about changing round the roles each of us filled. I resigned as Managing Director and promoted myself to Chairman – and made several other changes that left people rather stunned, having had several months of quietly getting on with what they had always done. There wasn't much in my vision about me personally, except, "It will take a year – and there is something else for you to do."

This vision had a lot of gaps in it, and I certainly was not used to receiving things like that in my rather ordinary Christian life as a member of an Anglican church, even though it was quite a lively bible-believing church. But there was no doubt that I had received *something*, even though there were no words written down for me, only pictures of situations that required me to act to bring them about, with mere glimpses of what might happen in the future when I took this action.

The process did indeed take a year, and a year that turned out to be very exciting for the company. There was a financial crisis that was absolutely nail-biting at the time, but resulted in a company that was much better based than before – and also left me with a picture that remains clearly etched in my mind.

The new Managing Director, specifically appointed by God as far as I was concerned, was lying in a ward in a Sussex hospital, stretched out with no clothes on, surrounded by fans to keep his body temperature down, having stopped breathing at least twice the night before. It terrified his wife, and certainly worried me, as here was the man on whom the future of the company rested, but who was seemingly near to death. I remember thinking, "Lord, you're cutting this really fine. Do you *really* know what you're doing?"

It wasn't the last time I cried out this thought to God over the next few years and on this occasion, as on all the others, all was well. The key company man recovered fully from what was apparently an infection related to bird-seed!

Meanwhile, as far as my colleagues were concerned, I was working myself out of a job. "What are you going to do?" was a common question. "Oh, there are plans," was my reply, thinking all the while, "I wish you'd let me know what they are Lord … and soon please!"

I found it frustrating to be questioned about the precise nature of this "vision," because I simply did not have an answer. It seemed that it was going to be left to us to flesh out the details and the only part that was made clear was the immediate next step, and this we had to take in faith.

Mary and I were Pathfinder leaders and had enjoyed taking our group of youngsters away for weekends, and found these times were really helpful. Maybe this was something we could develop, we thought, with a farmhouse and barn in the country, and bunks for a dozen or so to stay.

A house near us in Sussex came up for sale and prompted some further thoughts along these lines. But Sussex was fairly expensive. Should we consider further afield? And so the search began.

It is interesting, looking back, how often the Lord has thrown thought-provoking clues of his will for my life at me. As a teenager, I was taken with a school group to Capernwray Hall in Lancashire, and experienced the presence of the Lord in worship and teaching. Christian Conference Centres seemed fascinating places! I also remember on another occasion seeing an old car parked in The High, Oxford with the name "Dorcas" carefully painted on the side of its bonnet. "Dorcas ... full of good works" (Acts 9:36, KJV). The Lord obviously knows well my interest in cars, and also my weakness for terrible jokes. So, for a while our 'project' was known as the Dorcas Project, as we sensed that somehow mechanical things were going to be involved.

This led us further on in our search. Both Mary and I had been involved in West Runton Camps, an organisation that had started with a Christian canvas camp for young people on the cliff top at West Runton in North Norfolk. It was now running activities in several other locations under the name Dolphin Camps, and included a Go-Kart camp which used airfields in Norfolk at whatever location the MOD would allow – often at very short notice - each year. This activity badly needed a permanent base. Perhaps our Dorcas Project could provide this?

Norfolk, and East Anglia in general, certainly provided good value for money in property terms, and was in a sense our spiritual home. Fairly soon, estate agents' particulars started arriving in each post, and eventually we had looked at around two hundred – but none seemed right.

Letton Hall came up early on, in response to a phone call from an estate agent who had seen that there was an airfield nearby, which he thought might be used as a Go-Kart track. We duly turned up to view, unusually as a full family of five, with Jonathan (17), Simon (16) and Bridget (12), as well as Mary and me. The property was much too big! Way beyond our vision of a farmhouse with barn for twelve bunks. Nevertheless, we persevered through the three-hour tour (instead of the half hour we were prepared for) and as soon as we were in the car and out of earshot, burst into laughter. It really did seem ridiculously over-sized.

Letton Hall from above.

We looked at many other properties around East Anglia, and I became so well-informed that I often knew what was on the market before the estate agents did, but nothing seemed right. We heard that, in any case, Letton Hall had been sold to someone else, and then later that it was no longer on the market for other reasons. We started to feel we'd got it wrong somewhere, so we looked elsewhere in the country – but still nothing.

But then we had a phone call to ask if we might still be interested in Letton Hall, because the owner, Mrs Elizabeth Eglington, "had liked what she'd heard of our plans" and the property was still available. We looked again. It was still as big as we remembered ... but could it be right?

Letton Hall.

Meanwhile, we were feeling that if we were to take the Lord in any way seriously, we had better consider selling our house in Sussex. Such was the state of the market at that time that before it had been advertised at all, two families were competing to buy it – and our faith was greatly challenged. It was all going much too quickly for us.

Another of the moments etched onto my memory was kneeling in an upstairs room, praying, and then signing the sale agreement, knowing that unless we found somewhere else to live soon it would mean the entire family would be homeless, including my mother, two dogs and two cats, let alone Mary and me and three teenage children. It was another example of the Lord only giving us the next step and no more. But it seemed that from the moment we signed away our security, everything started to move forward on the Letton Hall front.

The West Runton team agreed that it could provide a Go-Kart camp base and, although it was very big, the accommodation might work very well as a holiday and activities centre. I asked a local surveyor to carry out as thorough a survey as he could for £200, and although he produced four pages of problems, it wasn't all bad news. Was Letton Hall the right place after all? We decided to make an offer to see what happened. This was another moment that I remember well, because we went for a cup of tea in a Wymondham teashop after visiting Letton again, and having come to a decision as we sat down, I phoned the offer in between ordering the tea and its arrival.

At the time all this was happening, I had been reading through the Living Bible paraphrase, starting at Genesis and working through the whole bible, day by day, chapter by chapter in order, more or less as circumstances permitted, without any particular timetable. On October 7th 1978 I had reached 2 Chronicles and found myself reading chapter 7, verse 10:

Then, on October 7, [Solomon] sent the people home, joyful and happy because the Lord had been so good ... [v12] The Lord appeared to Solomon and told him, "I have heard your prayer and have chosen this Temple as the place ..."[v16] I have chosen this Temple and sanctified it to be my home for ever; my eyes and my heart shall always be here.

It didn't really matter to me that day whether or not the Living Bible was accurate in the dates it quoted, but it said in black and white "October 7" and I was reading it on October 7th. It certainly caught my attention! And I also knew that I had been praying earnestly for the Lord to show me whether Letton Hall was the right place, and here he was, saying (albeit in different circumstances) "this is the place I have chosen." I found it very compelling.

As if to leave me with no escape, Savills wrote on Monday October 8th to say that the family had accepted our offer "over the weekend," and it's difficult not to think that they did this on October 7th. I was convinced! The Lord was putting his seal on Letton Hall.

The stable block at Letton.

We completed the purchase of Letton Hall on November 30th, having completed the sale of our Sussex house on November 5th. So we *were* actually homeless for nearly a month, but arrangements went well. And we did actually have the money without having to arrange a mortgage (there was even a surplus of £930.16, although that soon went on extra expenses!) I couldn't even wriggle out of the deal by saying we didn't have the money.

So Letton it had to be. The Lord had located his workshop.

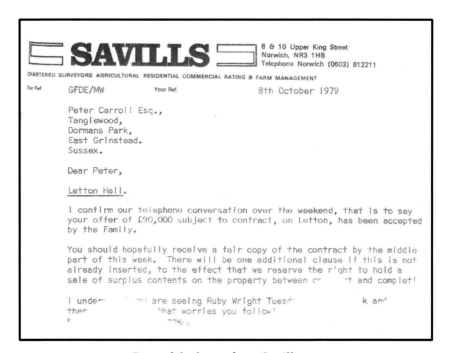

SAVILLS

8 & 10 Upper King Street
Norwich, NR3 1HB
Telephone Norwich (0603) 612211

Our Ref. GFDE/MW   Your Ref.   8th October 1979

Peter Carroll Esq.,
Tanglewood,
Dormans Park,
East Grinstead.
Sussex.

Dear Peter,

Letton Hall.

I confirm our telephone conversation over the weekend, that is to say
your offer of £90,000 subject to contract, on Letton, has been accepted
by the Family.

You should hopefully receive a fair copy of the contract by the middle
part of this week. There will be one additional clause if this is not
already inserted, to the effect that we reserve the right to hold a
sale of surplus contents on the property between c⌐   ⌐t and complet⌐

I under⌐   ⌐ou are seeing Ruby Wright Tuesd⌐   k an⌐
ther   ⌐hat worries you follo⌐⌐
⌐   ⌐⌐⌐⌐

*Part of the letter from Savills
telling us our offer had been accepted.*

CHAPTER THREE

THE FIRST SIX MONTHS

Saturday December 1st 1979, the day we moved in, was quite mild. We walked around the outside of the house in the early evening, dressed in shirtsleeves, looking up at the high walls, thinking with nervous anticipation, "Just what have we done?" For many months I preferred looking at the house only in moonlight, when the soft glow hid all the maintenance problems that were lying in wait.

The task of moving in proved something of an adventure in itself. We had decided to do it without professional help, using our own company vans plus Range Rover and car-transporter trailer. On one journey towards the end of the process, our upright piano was loaded onto the trailer and, as we arrived at Letton, we took the tarpaulin cover off and played our way in up the drive! Aside from lighter moments such as this, it was a lot of hard work.

Another instance that sticks in my mind speaks of the tangible presence of the Holy Spirit. I was driving a fully loaded van up the A11 one evening when I was overcome with an inexplicable sense of God's presence and found myself singing and praising him at the top of my voice; not a normal experience for me when driving company vans! Although we subsequently became used to occasions such as this, it caught me by surprise as I moved out of commercial, and into Christian "business."

One of the first communications to be sent out was an appeal for prayer as we came to terms with the mammoth task. Eighty-eight rooms, almost all needing decorating; also twelve loos, eight showers, twelve washbasins, all needed installation urgently. A job advert went out for any "Bezalels" who might come and help. (Exodus 35:30ff: "Bezalel - a man ... filled with the Spirit of God, with skill, ability and knowledge in all kinds of crafts.")

Although the real work in the Lord's workshop was to be a spiritual one, all the practical details had to be in place too. We needed tools and equipment. An early arrival was Fergy, a 1960(ish) Ferguson diesel tractor, who arrived tied up with a large red crepe paper ribbon as a present for Mary from the family on Christmas Day, 1979. Simon and I had proudly collected it from Beccles on the car-transporter trailer, in answer to an advertisement, but Mary was understandably uncertain how to regard this gift! In any case, Fergy proved very hard to start for the next few months, but eventually became an essential part of the team and, to date, has continued to serve well for nearly thirty-five years.

Tim Nicholson on Fergy.

Individuals and work parties responded to our appeals, initially tending to come from West Runton teams and Pathfinder groups, and from our own church in Sussex. There was much to do, indoors and out, painting, clearing rubble, building giant bonfires, and getting ready for groups to come and stay from May 1980 onwards. We began to realise there was tremendous fellowship to be enjoyed in the apprentices' workshop.

Another task that needed to be tackled urgently was dry rot. We knew that it was present before we purchased Letton Hall (in fact, its presence had deterred some prospective buyers altogether), but Rentokil had carried out four man-days of survey and had estimated "£1500 certainly, possibly going up to £5000" of work. A small team arrived and fairly soon discovered at least one cause: a bath waste pipe disappearing through a wall, apparently to a corresponding pipe outside, but the two pipes were not connected and water had been pouring into the brickwork for a long time!

Dry rot: Be careful when pulling the chain in case it all comes down ...

The Rentokil team continued to find more incidences of dry rot, not only in the old kitchen area of the Hall, but also in the north-east corner of the bedroom floors, immediately adjacent to work they had previously carried out for the Eglingtons, the former owners. Their demolition work certainly provided plenty of rubble for the work parties to remove and, according to instruction, take out in sealed bags, avoiding further contamination from the spores. Any infected wood also had to be burnt. After a few months of this, the Rentokil bill amounted to around £20,000 and we had to say "enough." They left by the end of May 1980. Settling this much-larger-than-expected bill cast a shadow over Letton's finances for a long time.

We had learnt how to recognise dry rot by the time the experts left, and its recurrence and the need to be ruthless in removing it became a constant worry over the next few years, and even up to the present time. It seems to be like cancer in a building. If left unchecked, it becomes fatal as all infected cellulose material (mainly wood) is destroyed and the structure collapses. And just when you think you've got rid of it, new infected areas turn up. Like cancer in people, it brought us to real tears on a number of occasions.

Work party jobs for all ages.

The house needed furnishing of course, and the furniture we had brought with us barely filled one corner. We became regular visitors to the Watton Sale Rooms and the auctioneer soon got into the habit of turning to us expectantly whenever beds or chairs etc were obviously not going to attract bids from more discerning customers. Mary was our regular bidder at the auctions and the rest of us would wait eagerly for her return each week to see what she had "won" this time.

Gradually, the place began to look less empty. The West Runton Kart Camps had built up a stock of dining tables, dining chairs and general kitchen equipment over preceding years, by virtue of having to set up camp in whatever airfield the Ministry of Defence allocated them each year, and this was made available to Letton. And so the one-time-elegant Drawing Room became the house party kitchen. What would Sir John Soane and the titled previous owners of Letton have made of this, we wondered.

Working on the old lily pond, under the direction of Sarah.

The incentive for Kart Camp teams to be involved was the prospect of having their own track. Could it be constructed in time? There was less than six months to go. We sought advice and assistance from as many sources as we could think of, including the Cement and Concrete Association, the army, various contractors, and even the Beaulieu National Motor Museum, but the general answer was, "No, we can't help."

So, the only remaining option was to do it ourselves. I remember daring to pray that we could, with Mary and I and Tony Collis kneeling beside our sofa. Tony was a GP in Worcester and had set up and equipped the Kart Camps largely through his own personal generosity and commitment, and was equally supportive of Letton Hall, from its very beginning and into its future development. His help was invaluable at this stage of Letton's life and continues still, despite the long commute between Worcester and Norfolk.

A work party taking a tea break,
with Mary Carroll second from the left.

The track was designed by an impressive team of experts (including a professor of engineering, a surveyor, a doctor, and sundry other engineers), with the basic criterion being that the faster the karts were going, the further they should be from solid objects such as walls and trees. The site selected was the old shrubbery garden, with brick walls and gardeners' buildings and cowsheds scattered around. We also discovered a deep water tank concealed just under the surface - an interesting hazard for racing go-karts.

Work began in March, clearing the site, excavating the track and filling it in with compacted hard-core. The call went out to volunteer work parties that "June is Concrete Time – only 100mm thick, but 1000 square metres big." There were twenty-seven bays in all, with my eldest son Jonathan as Resident Site Engineer, coordinating workers and concrete deliveries. It was an important and key responsibility, and Jonathan was my right-hand man in so much of Letton's development at this time.

Constructing the kart track.

To our great delight and with a real sense of achievement, the track was completed in time for the first Kart Camp, and opened formally on 25th July 1980 by the Bishop of Norwich, Maurice Wood, whose picture made the front page of the Eastern Daily Press the following day. Bishop Maurice also unveiled the words cast into the concrete at the entrance to the kart-track:

ISAIAH 40: 3- 4   A ROAD FOR THE LORD

Bishop Maurice Wood opens the kart track
and draws attention to the inscription.

A bird's eye view of the construction site.

Bishop Maurice receives instruction from Jonathan Carroll, with Dr Tony Collis overseeing things from behind.

As apprentices in the Lord's workshop, one hopes that one's work will be remembered in spiritual terms and perhaps many pious memories, but so often visitors to Letton Hall only seem to have remembered the go-karts! Hopefully, the full wording of the inscription goes some way towards bridging the gap:

In the desert prepare the way for the Lord; make straight in the wilderness a highway for our God. Every valley shall be raised up, every mountain and hill made low; the rough ground shall become level, the rugged places a plain. And the glory of the Lord will be revealed ...

BISHOP TAKES TO THE KART TRACK

A cheerful wave from the Bishop of Norwich, the Rt. Rev. Maurice Wood, as he sets off on a go-kart after opening the new track at the Letton Hall Christian Youth holiday centre last night. Report, page 13.

Headline news: The bishop takes to the track.

Bishop's go-kart lap of honour

The Bishop of Norwich, the Rt. Rev. Maurice Wood, opened Letton Hall Christian Youth Holiday Centre's go-kart track last night — and then braved the track in a lap of honour.

The concrete track has been laid by volunteers at the centre, which is run by Mr. Peter Carroll as the Letton Hall Trust. His son, Jonathan, has been responsible for much of the work on the track.

West Runton Dolphin Camps, who are part of the Scripture Union, hope to make Letton Hall a regular centre, making full use of the track. At present they have 34 boys, between 13 and 16, and 17 officers on a two-week holiday there.

The Bishop arrived with his lay chaplain, Mr. Bob Drayson, at the main hall entrance, where he was met by the West Runton camp commandant, Dr. Tony Collis, the camp adjutant, Mr. John Whitfield, and the technical director, Mr. David Bryant.

After touring the main hall, library and dining room, the Bishop viewed a display of electronics projects undertaken by the young people, and watched an aero-modelling display in the Dolphin Court area of the centre.

The bishop gave a short address and prayer before formally declaring the track open and cutting a red tape. An inscription on the surface was then revealed from Isaiah: "A road for the Lord."

He then took to the track for a lap of honour, followed by a cavalcade of boys in the remaining go-karts.

Mr. Carroll's aim is to convert all buildings at Letton Hall into a self-contained Christian activities and holiday centre for young people.

Mr. Carroll's wife, Mary, who devoted much time in the initial stages of setting up the centre, died last month.

Letton Hall, built between 1785 and 1788 by Sir John Soane, was a private home until the Carrolls moved in last year from Kent.

Restoration work is being done as money permits. Removing dry rot and death watch beetle alone has cost £20,000.

CHAPTER FOUR

BEREAVEMENT

My wife Mary had been fully involved in the planning and early stages of work on the kart track, as well as all the other tasks that needed to be done. She was a very capable person, having trained as an Occupational Therapist at Oxford and been involved in pioneering domiciliary OT work in Sussex before we left. She came from a high-achieving Savage family background and was a discerning director of our own business – and through her role in the developing Letton Hall project, she had been in the forefront as the West Runton organisation began to involve women more in a previously male-dominated climate.

Mary Carroll

Our family had moved into the Courtyard Flat in February and my mother, known to everyone as Gran, moved into a bed-sit within it shortly afterwards, so there was a lot of home-making to do. Both Mary and Gran followed bravely as we worked out the vision.

On May 5th, the day before her 42nd birthday, Mary had been cutting the grass in the walled garden, using the ride-on mower which we had bought locally, when she came in and collapsed on the floor of our sitting room. She had been having occasional stomach cramps for some time, including a couple of bouts during our family holiday a few weeks earlier, but nothing that seemed very serious. The pains had been put down to an unidentified dietary problem up until now.

This time it was clearly much worse. The local GP, Dr Dickie, realising she had lost a lot of blood, set up a drip and summoned an ambulance urgently. As Mary was being carried out of our bedroom she looked around it and said, "I wonder if I will come back here again...?" I didn't know what to make of that remark at the time, but it certainly stuck in my mind. What did she mean? Did she feel we should move to a different room when she returned? Or was she thinking much more seriously? Anyway, I dismissed it. "Don't be silly!" I think I probably said.

That night, she underwent an emergency operation, from which I was to understand later that she only barely survived. I was slowly coming to terms with the situation and spent the next three days in a kind of surreal daze – but it was an intensely spiritual time when I felt the close presence of the Lord in a way that I never had before. I went through many what-ifs, as if the Lord was gently preparing me for whatever was to come.

All seemed to go well immediately after the operation, with tests indicating no malignancy, even though the surgeon who had carried out the operation could not agree, and tried to tell me that what he had seen led him to believe it was serious cancer.

40

Mary spent around three weeks in the Norfolk and Norwich Hospital but didn't seem to recover her health as hoped. One interesting aspect, however, was that for some time she was under the special nursing care of a young Christian nurse called Kay Nundy, and the two of them discussed this project of Letton Hall. According to Kay, her heart "leapt within her" when she heard about it.

I was visiting Mary daily, keeping her up-to-date with, among other things, progress on the kart track with Jonathan's reports on how many bays had been worked on, so I too met Kay. How gracious of God to allow my first wife to introduce me to my future wife in such a way that I was fully provided for – although I had absolutely no idea of this at the time, of course!

But Mary's progress was slow and she was continuing to lose weight rapidly. The Norwich medical team, in consultation with the family, decided that she should move to Addenbrookes Hospital in Cambridge but there were problems with bed availability and ambulance transport at that time. To speed up the process, Mary's brother Michael and I took her to Cambridge by car, realising in doing so just how ill and frail she had become. We settled her in the Evelyn Nursing Home, close to the hospital, where she could be seen by the Addenbrookes consultant without having to wait for a hospital bed to become available.

The prognosis was not good, but we agreed to allow him to carry out a course of chemotherapy. One of my main memories of this time was pushing Mary around the grounds in a wheelchair, having just received the consultant's views and talking together about it, but thinking all the time that this happens to other people. Not to us.

My faith was absolutely firm at this time. Mary was not going to die. I think one knows when one is bolstering up one's faith, trying to put on a confident face when actually one is not completely sure inside. But my faith was completely solid, which was a real blessing, because it meant I could never blame myself when Mary died, thinking, "If only I had had more faith."

But Mary did die, after only a couple of weeks in Cambridge, and by now in the hospital itself. Sadly, the effects of strong chemotherapy so affected her body chemistry that she was in a permanent coma for the last week of her life. Interestingly though, when I and the nurse attending Mary were bending over her head, and the nurse closed her eyes finally, there was no sense of defeat in me or any sense of blaming God. I felt a peace from the Lord, although also a measure of serious panic on a human level.

Mary and Jonathan

In announcing her death, in a note to Letton supporters, I said, "Letton has lost housekeeper, policy-maker, bookings administrator, secretary, book-keeper and 'getter-of-things-done' - at least ..."

I had no sense that the Letton venture should finish, but said in the note, "I have a fellow feeling with the Corinthians when Paul pointed out that 'we walk by faith, not by sight' – but long for a glimpse ahead! So many of the plans we had made have been knocked sideways that all we can do is fall to our knees ..."

Mary was buried in the churchyard of Letton's parish church in Cranworth, and the words on her headstone are for me a constant encouragement and reminder of the Christian's confidence in life after death - so I need not be concerned for Mary, and had only to come to terms with the changes in my own life. I came to recognise that marriage is a human institution but that the loss for Mary's children was in one sense much greater. Our first summer holiday without her and with me as a single parent was hard for us all to cope with.

Mary's death brought the Letton Hall project into a whole new phase. No longer was it something of a family venture. It was now something much wider.

Mary's headstone - "with her Lord in Glory."

CHAPTER FIVE

THE WORKSHOP OPENS

Up until June 1980, visitors to Letton Hall were almost entirely work parties or individuals coming to help develop the work in some practical way. From July onwards, there was a steady change in emphasis. This quote from the visitors' book is from a small group of early visitors from a North London church, who came in August to "get a broader view":

The beauty of the country – the love in Letton Hall - the grace and favour in all the rooms – all pointed our fellowship in the direction of our Lord – and we rejoiced. Rejoice in the Lord always, and again I say rejoice.

Letton Hall, open to all.

Over the next eighteen months, until the end of 1981, around fifty groups came, almost all with the aim of spending time in fellowship with each other and the Lord. We didn't refuse any offers of work of course, but were pleased to see the Lord at work in the visitors rather than the visitors at work in Letton. This was truly the Lord's workshop opening up, we felt.

This university group was one of several visiting Letton, as the workshop opened up.

The West Runton organisation came regularly, using the newly constructed kart track of course, but with wider Christian aims than merely karting. Youth groups came from nearby and from distant places, and church and university groups heard about us and visited. One memorable occasion was when the Magdalene

College, Cambridge CU Executive Committee arrived and occupied Letton in true country-house style, including candlelit dinner on the terrace. "Carols at Letton" over Christmas 1981 started a tradition that lasted for many years to come, with large scale decorations initially introduced to cover up peeling paint and cracks in the plaster. The Navigators organisation brought groups, and the first of our school groups arrived, brought by their Christian teachers who had heard about us.

But apart from the many blessings we were experiencing, there were other aspects that needed addressing. There was a "Business Meeting no.1" held over the weekend of 5-7th December 1980, including people who had become involved, and who wanted to help to ensure the project continued successfully. They included representatives of the organisations using Letton Hall, as well as residents and supporters in general. The agenda was far-reaching and enabled all the key issues to be explored and all the searching questions to be asked and freely discussed - and the resulting full and lively correspondence lasted for several weeks afterwards.

Another similar meeting was held in March 1981, and it was indicative of the level of support that when it came to drawing up a list for a suggested management committee, thirty names came readily to mind – all experienced and able people. In the end, a "Task Force 81" was set up, led by five key people, resident at Letton, and covering all aspects of management, administration and practical work. This plan is summarised in Letton News no.5 (Appendix 1, p.155).

Money was of course a key issue and up to this point my personal resources, as owner of Letton, had been at the heart of the situation - but others had been very generous. A West Runton Dolphin Camps Appeal was launched to help improve the facilities, as well as the Mary Carroll Memorial Fund, to provide some lasting recognition of her role in starting up Letton. Finances were clearly going to be vital in the future (as later chapters show), but at this early stage every gift, from the smallest to the greatest, brought us enormous encouragement.

This extract from Letton News no.5 (January 1981) paints an exciting but rather humbling picture:

Already many needs have been met – just look at the list below:

- *The WEST RUNTON DOLPHIN CAMPS APPEAL has now raised more than £9000*
- *The MARY CARROLL MEMORIAL FUND now stands at £2700*
- *£100 collection from a service arranged and conducted by a CYFA Group in their church*
- *£50 in an envelope – with no further comment*
- *£10 from someone who had won a Youth Award and wanted Letton to share it*
- *£500 from a missionary family serving overseas*
- *£10 from an octogenarian OAP*
- *£200 from a small group of young people, who had raised it through a Garage Sale*
- *£50 given from a Christmas Bonus – "Letton helped me to work to earn it"*
- *£100 cheque in an envelope which just said "Philippians 4:19" – nothing more*
- *£100 plus – given a few pounds at a time – by Pathfinders towards the 'Halle-loo-jah' Project*
- *£150 from a sponsored Bike Ride by Pathfinders*
- *£400 from a Pathfinder weekend.*

All those involved could see the blessings that the Lord was piling on visitors coming to Letton, and were committed to what was clearly a venture of faith. But it had to be faith, not foolishness. One supporter, a surgeon by profession, cut to the core of the situation in a letter to me saying, "Many of us thought you had very much more private means than is apparent ... If you were a millionaire there would be money to see us through ..." He did add, though, that everyone seemed

united in the terms of Hebrews 10:19-25: "We have confidence …
let us encourage one another."

One of the things that really did encourage everyone was the
large number of people who volunteered their help. In my
personal comments in Letton News no.7 (October 1981) I
expressed thanks to Tony Collis, Sonia Knight, Don Gee, Philip
Doyne and all the Lettoneers - as well as to the London
Advisory Group (irreverently known as the old LAGs), led by
John Collins. I was grateful for the backing of the Appeal
Trustees, including Clive and Kristen Whalley and Geoffrey
Bond, and for the support of Richard and Trish Millard and the
West Runton family, and also my many friends from Felbridge
church. But I also gave a flavour of my personal life at Letton
with a self-portrait of myself at my desk - with the footnote that
I regretted how accurate it was!

CHAPTER SIX

THERE IS ALWAYS COMPANY

One of the things that sent me into something of a panic after Mary died was the thought that I was on my own now. How on earth was I going to cope? My mistake, of course, was to think of it in earthly terms. The Lord soon presented me with what seemed to be a continuous stream of people appearing over the horizon.

One example will perhaps help to illustrate. Just a few days after Mary's funeral, I was hiding away in the house of some friends while they were away, getting some time to myself, when the phone rang. Although I didn't think anyone knew where I was (I hardly knew myself, at that stage), the call was for me. Apparently the principals of a bible college in Cambridge were looking for a property to use in Norfolk, and the specification looked as if it would fit Letton Hall. The intermediary who had phoned me wondered if it might be helpful to meet.

They visited Letton and, although nothing came of it in the end, it caught my attention, because the property specification had been drawn up more than a year previously, and put out in their prayer letter at that time "for future consideration." Only around the time of Mary's death had it become a current matter. I thought to myself, "If God has been planning things in advance like this, taking matters in account before I even reached there myself, perhaps I need not worry so much. He knew my needs before I even had them."

Many friends rallied round, from my old church and from the new local ones I had now established links with, and from the

West Runton organisation. Tony Collis was "Deputy Squire" and a staunch friend and co-worker, and of course, I was surrounded by family. But I still missed the constant presence of Mary.

Gradually, a team built up. Young people came along, keen to help, perhaps between school and university, or before or between jobs. Others came along whenever they could fit in a weekend or so alongside their professional work - and we came up with the name "Lettoneers" to encompass this vital resource. They came with an amazing range of skills and abilities, some on a long-term residential basis and others as short-term Lettoneers. The old kitchen area in the cellars became their base and social focus, with the main hall AGA brought down and re-assembled to provide warmth and a cooking facility there.

The Lettoneers relaxing in the Library.

Some of these early Lettoneers need to be mentioned here as their names and contributions keep on recurring in the Letton story. Andrew Whadcoat and Tim Nicholson, both working for the BBC, and teacher David Morgan, brought many technical skills to bear as the project developed. Kay also came as a Lettoneer, having volunteered to Mary to provide convalescent nursing, but elected to come and give general help even when it was clear that Mary would no longer need nursing.

Lettoneers, on show and having fun at Shipdham Fete with a float on the theme of 'Upstairs and Downstairs'.

Sonia Knight arrived in November 1980 and provided administrative and home-making help. With her labrador Bundle, she became a focus for the family of Lettoneers and for the growing number of groups visiting. Her practical and spiritual contribution was absolutely vital during her involvement, which lasted for more than five years. Some more details are included in Appendix 2 (p.156).

Very early on in our residence at Letton, two local ladies appeared at the front door to our flat, looking rather apprehensive and asking if this was some kind of Christian Centre. They were standing rather close together, as if they were secretly holding hands for mutual support, but had heard rumours in the village and felt they wanted to find out more. This was a truly historic meeting, although none of us had any idea of this at the time.

One lady was June Rootham, whose involvement with Letton is described later. The other was Enid Roberts, who was to become absolutely key to the operation of Letton for the next twenty-seven years. Perhaps if she had known that she would have been less eager to call! She became administrator, secretary, the person in charge of bookings, and generally the public face and first point of contact for all visitors. Her generous and gentle style of service set the scene at Letton. For more than two years in the 1980s, she and her husband Alan lived-in as resident wardens, but eventually she retired at the end of 2007 (see Appendix 3, p.157), despite repeated efforts over previous years to persuade her to stay. But even as she left her retirement party, her words were, "See you on Tuesday," signifying her intention to return as a volunteer. Sadly, Enid died in a road accident early in 2009.

Enid's husband Alan was the man with miracles at his fingertips, not only with his chosen field of motor vehicles but with any of the myriad of technical problems and challenges thrown at him by Letton. His imaginative solutions helped us through many difficulties and his patience and persistence saved the day on many occasions. But his talents were not limited to the technical. After a while, a pattern showed itself, so that whenever someone worked alongside Alan for any significant time they became a Christian. His quiet practical witness was a special corner of the Lord's workshop, and Alan's well-thumbed bible one of the key tools.

One particular occasion combined Alan's practical skills with his ability to encourage Christian discipleship. The Baptist Missionary Organisation were looking for a place where one of their trainee missionaries could gain some practical skills before being sent to Zaire, and although we had mixed feelings about being chosen as a place where third-world conditions could be experienced at first hand, we agreed to accept Richard.

Alan chose a project for him to work on, which he thought would be suitable for someone who didn't as yet have much technical expertise, and set him to work restoring an ancient water pump. Eventually, after a bit of a struggle, Richard managed to get the pump working, alongside doing other work around Letton, and displayed it proudly.

After a month or two, he was sent off to his posting in Africa and I have the impression that he was met with a sense of urgency directly off the plane by a worried local man who said they had a major problem and hoped Richard would be able to help. The water supply had failed in an outlying area and urgent action was desperately needed. They duly went out to investigate and to Richard's amazement, the fault lay in a water pump which was exactly the same model as the ancient one he had worked on at Letton! All was fixed, Richard's reputation grew by leap and bounds, and the next thing we heard was that he was setting up all the technical aspects of an operating theatre. It was a fascinating exercise for us to realise just how amazingly the Lord could use his workshop. And perhaps it was an instance of the Lord's sense of humour too!

Geoff Sussex visited Letton in early 1981 to see whether it was a suitable venue to which to bring members of his Baptist church. He concluded it wasn't, but we chatted together as we walked to his car.

"We have a lot of work to do to the place, as you can see – particularly with the plumbing," I said.

An interesting look came over his face and he said, "I used to be a plumber before I became a Baptist minister."

My attention was caught, and I immediately started sounding out the situation. Geoff admitted that in fact his diary had an unexpected three-month gap in it, which was puzzling him.

"But I couldn't consider any work at Letton, because I would need a mate and I don't have one."

We parted, with me desperately disappointed as I walked back up to the office. The phone was ringing, and someone called Paul was wondering if he could help at Letton.

"I'm a painter," he said, so I started to talk about the number of rooms we needed to decorate.

"Actually, I'm not that sort of painter," he said, "I'm a Fine Arts graduate."

So ended another of my dreams, but I asked Paul if there was anything else he did.

"No, not really. Oh, I did used to help my father a bit … he was a plumber."

We had our plumber's mate, and Geoff and Paul worked together for many months installing pipe work. Our Lord recruited his apprentices and looked after them in a truly wonderful way!

CHAPTER SEVEN

OWNING THE WORKSHOP

The Letton Hall project started out as a family project and the Carrolls were able to purchase the workshop property from their own resources, but soon began to wonder whether the venture should be put on a more formal basis. After discussion, Alastair Watson, a solicitor with Lewis and Dick, drew up deeds for the Letton Hall Trust and on 17th March 1980, the deed was signed and the trust came into being.

On advice, the terms were very broad, being primarily, "The advancement of the Christian faith, either in the United Kingdom or overseas," but the title identified it as related to Letton. The first trustees were Mary and me, so it was still very much a family affair, but as Charitable Trust no.279817, registered with the Charity Commission, it had a legal existence of its own.

We considered transferring ownership of the property to the trust, but this didn't seem the best way and there were a number of complications. It was to be our own home as well as the base for the trust, and also my mother had contributed to the purchase and her interests needed to be protected too. A further factor, and one which remained as a thorn in our sides for many years to come, was that our Sussex house had been used as back-up security for our company's dealings with the banks, and this charge had been carried forward to apply to our ownership of Letton. It was merely a 'just-in-case' security and would only have been called on if the company failed to meet its obligations. It would have been good to remove this charge from the start, but banks never like to let go of any of either belts or braces that they have managed to acquire and anyway, at the time it seemed relatively innocuous.

Leasing part of Letton Hall to the trust seemed the best way to go and discussions started immediately; but we became aware of another problem at this stage. When we purchased Letton, we had included a clause in the conveyance at the request of the vendors, which allowed them first refusal if we came to sell the property. Since they owned and farmed all the land around Letton, this seemed a sensible arrangement and once again, an innocuous clause. However, the clause not only covered an outright sale but also the situation where we "otherwise disposed of" the property, and this included leasing Letton Hall to the trust.

Letton's extensive property was suitable for dividing up.
This is my favourite aerial photograph, taken by David Ham
and used with permission.

This clause would also have come into effect if we chose to sell just part of Letton. Tony Collis and Sonia Knight pursued this idea by a scheme to purchase Dolphin Court and develop and operate it in conjunction with the main hall, but although it would have helped the finances, and was a very generous offer, it was not followed up.

The Eglingtons, from whom we had bought Letton, had always had differing views within the family about selling the property. They were faced with substantial death duties and such a large house was no longer needed now that most members of the family had moved out. At the time of purchase, only Mrs Lizzie Eglington lived in the main hall, with her daughter Catherine living in the Courtyard flat.

Chris and Bruce Eglington, who ran the main farm, saw advantages in selling the property to raise funds and provide additional capital for expansion, but their father Derek had been vehemently opposed to the sale from the start. He farmed two hundred acres nearby, but didn't seem to be a farmer by first choice of career and would have probably have been an engineer if left to his own devices. But as the only son in a farming family, he had been thrust into the role.

There was a real concern, both on our part and on the part of other members of the family, that Derek Eglington, if offered the prospect of buying back Letton Hall, might just take it up. I asked him what he intended to do with the property if it became his. He said, "More-or-less what you are doing," which although perhaps being rather flattering, wasn't at all realistic. In any case, negotiations with his solicitors proved very difficult as they complained they could never contact him for instructions.

Meanwhile, the Letton Hall Trust was finding its finances increasingly tight, although more and more groups were visiting and finding blessing from the Lord. Moreover, the trust had only one trustee. The Charity Commissioners knew of this situation and were taking a benign view so far, but were obviously unhappy for this to continue for the long term. We needed more trustees and more money!

A key meeting took place on 1st December 1981, two years to the day from when we arrived at Letton. Here, the London Advisory Group said, with a very positive overview, that "this committee felt that the work had the marks of the Holy Spirit." We were still following up any financial schemes but, significantly, I was also able to report that "we had had an approach from a group of Christian men from Essex and North London who had been running house parties and camps for many years ... and who wanted to become involved with the responsibility for Letton and for raising finance."

Some of this group had already visited Letton, but one visit really stuck in my mind. Phil Webb said he had heard the name Letton mentioned twice in recent days, and had then found himself only a few miles away when an appointment was cancelled and he had a few hours free. He thought perhaps he should visit this place he had heard about so recently.

I remember meeting him and, after showing him around, praying with him and saying to the Lord, "I don't think either Phil or I know what this is all about, but it seems to have your hand in it." This was one of those God-incidences that convinced me that the Lord was moving us on to the next stage. Another indication was that although everyone involved had very busy diaries, we were able to agree a date to meet up together in the near future.

In Letton News no.7, sent out around this time, the heading was "Seek first His kingdom, Matthew 6:33", and I added my own thought that, "I feel very strongly that there is a work of the Lord to be done at Letton, so I am expecting to find a way opening up to enable this to happen ... Please pray for this aspect!"

CHAPTER EIGHT

TRUSTEES AND TEAM

On 30th December 1981, the new trustees were appointed and the next stage of the development of the Lord's workshop began. The trustees (with Appendix page references in brackets) were:

- Graham Arram, an engineer working with a district council, and secretary of the trust (p.160)
- Peter Carroll, resident at Letton Hall and the founding trustee (p.161)
- Garfield Jordan, an estate agent and surveyor, and chairman of the trust
- John Currey, an accountant and financial director, and treasurer of the trust (p.162)
- Gwyn Jordan, a university lecturer (p.163)
- Sonia Knight, resident at Letton Hall and administrator of the trust (p.156)
- Martin Lodge, a motor engineer (p.164)
- Phil Webb, a church minister (p.165)
- Pat Webb, a nurse, mother, and wife of Phil (p.165)

One of the first things the new trustees did was to adopt the maxim which had already been conceived: *Letton Hall - a house for the Lord*. This set the agenda for the future, and an Open Day was planned for 13th March 1982. The hope was that many more people would catch the vision, so that the trust could enlist the support of as many of them as possible. Information sheets and newsletters were produced and sent out, saying how this group of new trustees felt called by the Lord to take on the responsibilities of the project.

The work already carried out at Letton was acknowledged but "there were almost endless possibilities for further development," and a stated aim was to reach "Letton's full potential." The priority work included further improvements involving better heating and more decorating, and also necessary safety work.

One of the main aims of the trust – and in many ways, the over-riding one - was to purchase the property. It was agreed by everyone involved that if the trust owned Letton it would be a clearly understood situation, and easier for the trust to spend charitable money on a property they owned. Property prices were rising and if the trust owned Letton this would improve its financial position and provide stability for the future; but if it remained under family ownership, inheritance tax and other factors could make the situation uncertain.

Despite this agreement, somehow it didn't happen for thirty years! It certainly wasn't due to any reluctance on the part of the Carrolls to sell, nor was it due to any lack of effort or prayer by the trustees and supporters of Letton. So, it had to be the way the Lord intended it – but it was puzzling!

Money was one of the controlling factors. Appeals had failed to produce even a hopeful level of finance, and nor had any individual backer appeared to fund the purchase. The Carrolls couldn't afford merely to give the property away, since it was their home and in any case, the legal complications mentioned before could only be cleared by a sale. Several people who had been involved from early days and knew the situation urged the Carrolls to remain fully in the picture, since the vision had been given to me (Peter) in the first place – and it is interesting to note how ownership gives a special emphasis and a personal focus to involvement.

Typical of some of the comments we received was a letter from the director of an interdenominational Christian Centre, to whom Mary and I had first of all shared the vision the Lord had given, only days after the event. So, he had been in from the beginning. He had followed our progress, had visited Letton and met Kay and said, "God gave you the place and the vision ... and the job to get on with." We had shared the trust's and our own financial situation with him and he said, "So, in circumstances a Loving Father has permitted, you're both stuck there!"

No matter how everyone felt, and no matter how hard the Carrolls tried to get out, ownership by the trust became an unattainable goal and we all had to accept what seemed to be the Lord's will. The security of the whole venture was under-pinned by the increasing value of the property, which was rising by about 10% each year, so in one sense nothing was being wasted and all was being used in the Lord's work, no matter who owned Letton. It was truly a "House for the Lord" and we had to recognise that the Lord's timing was sovereign.

In the absence of immediate plans to purchase, the new trustees decided to continue with preparing a lease and, in June 1983, a first draft was submitted by Linda Coopersmith of Woodham Smith, the solicitors who had been acting for the Carrolls since before the purchase of Letton. Once again, however, it was not the straightforward task that had been envisaged and it was not until April 1999 that a final version was signed, after nearly sixteen years of negotiation!

Many factors had to be taken into account, all of them reasonable and understandable, but all of them requiring legal assistance, and the list of solicitors grew longer as the years passed. It included Lewis and Dick, Tony Wakeling, Ted Hubbard, Martin Jones and Hood Vores. The trust and the Charity Commissioners favoured a long lease of, say, twenty years, whereas banks and mortgage lenders preferred a shorter time of, say, two years, to protect their security. Somehow, the money spent by a charitable trust on property which wasn't their own needed to be protected, and also liability for repairs needed to be defined, with the spectres of a complete new roof or the collapse of the main staircase always looming as a worst case scenario.

The personal position of the trustees needed to be considered too, as they would be personally liable if the trust could not meet its obligations. The setting up of a Charitable Limited Company was embarked upon as a possible route to limit personal liability, but this route was not followed eventually. Also, there was the Option Agreement with the Eglingtons obstructing any kind of lease.

It is relatively easy to summarise this in a paragraph or two with the benefit of hindsight, but it took many hours of agenda time and reams of paper for letters and draft solutions etc, and was a major distraction from the real output of the Lord's workshop. It would have been altogether impossible to persevere were it not for the strength of the original vision and the ongoing blessing poured out by the Lord on visitors to Letton.

It was fairly typical of our experience at this time, as recorded in the minutes of the trustee meeting of 17th February 1983 that "the prevailing presence of the Holy Spirit reduced us to our knees ... and we committed the future of Letton to Him." We read from Isaiah 30: "In quietness and trust is your strength;" and from Luke 17: "When you have done everything you were told to do ... say 'we are unworthy servants; we have only done our duty.'"

One of the issues being grappled with at that time was the question of the Option Agreement, which was preventing us leasing. We had decided that we had to confront this problem head on, and on 17th February (the same date as the above trustee meeting), my solicitor sent a recorded delivery letter to the Eglingtons, offering to sell Letton to them for the most recent valuation figure of £310,000.

Once this offer had been made, a legal period of notice began. The clock was due to stop ticking at midnight on March 19th and to our consternation, Derek Eglington stated that he wished to take up the offer. So a great deal of focused prayer started! There were several side-issues that came into play, including efforts by Chris and Bruce to persuade their father to see sense, but the final outcome was a letter from Derek, dated 18th March, just one day before the deadline, saying that he wished to withdraw his name from the agreement. We had made the offer, they had not taken it up, and we were free to draw up a lease. Praise the Lord!

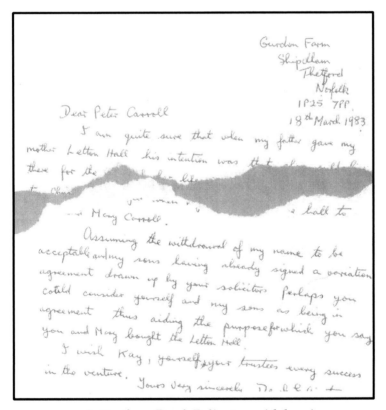

Letter from Derek Eglington withdrawing
from the Option Agreement.

THE TRUSTEES START TO BUILD A RESIDENT TEAM

One of the main effects of the new trustees joining the trust was that Phil and Pat came to live at Letton, after a short spell living nearby while their flat was "made ready." This was something of an optimistic term, as their accommodation was really very basic. It occupied part of the old male servants' wing and was known as The North Wing by those who had already stayed there, not so much for its actual location at Letton, more that it seemed to have a distinct similarity to the North Pole.

Having two of the new trustees permanently on site was a great encouragement to everyone one else resident there. It was agreed that Tony Collis need no longer commute regularly from his practice in Worcester, and also Peter Carroll could stand down from some of the duties he had been carrying out – which was extremely helpful because Peter and Kay married on 6th February 1982 (see later). The trustees decided that it would be a sensible idea if the custom followed for Jewish soldiers who married should be applied at Letton also, which was to take two years away from the battlefield. A generous provision!

We had at one time explored the concept of "community," where everyone would live together as one extended family, but had decided that it was better for Letton to be run by families living independently, but working together. So, with the arrival of Phil and Pat, there began a succession of resident couples to be neighbours of the Carrolls.

This marked the beginning of a subtle change in the pattern of life at Letton. The work and responsibilities were definitely 24/7 - round-the-clock and seven-days-a-week, with holidays even busier - and those people who were resident were aware of this and attempted to cover the situation. For them, Letton was a home and not merely a place at which they came to work. It was hard, but brought with it the ability to have a greater influence in Letton's operation and to experience greater personal fulfilment and satisfaction. As the number of visitors grew, it became clear that at least two resident couples were necessary, with the Carrolls being one of these, as the "senior family." Details of these key resident families are included in p.167-181 of the Appendices.

In a letter to me, Tim Nicholson gave his view of Letton Hall (from his experience as one of the earliest Lettoneers and also a key technical expert for many years). He called it: "'Integrated Christian living' – a home, a place of work (both spiritual and practical), a place of witness and a place of worship."

The Webbs moved out of Letton after nearly three years (although remaining as trustees) and Alan and Enid Roberts became resident wardens for two years. We then embarked on a refurbishing of the Norfolk Wing so that it could be ready for Stephen and Pippa Mawditt to join as managers in early 1988. Stephen's administrative and leadership abilities and Pippa's housekeeping skills were a great blessing to Letton Hall. Ken and Pat Webb (not the same Pat Webb!) arrived next in 1991, bringing with them many practical skills until, after three years, they moved out to their own house "Little Letton" in Watton.

Enid Roberts in the Letton office.

Next to make the Norfolk Wing their home were Gerald and June Rootham, and their stay was to be a long one. June, as mentioned earlier, was one of our first visitors in 1980 and they retired as managers in 2010, so their total involvement spanned thirty years. During the fifteen years they were resident, their impact on the life and operation of Letton Hall was enormous. Gerald's keen eye on cost savings and his personal and practical skills, together with June's hospitality and housekeeping gifts made them and their whole family a truly treasured asset. Many visitors experienced their Christian care and love for people, and Letton owes them a great debt. As was said during their time as managers, "with June and Gerald at the helm the Letton ship was in very safe hands."

Gerald and June Rootham.

Brian and Janet Adams and their family come in a rather different category to other resident families, because although they lived at Letton for ten months, one of their main purposes was to allow other residents to leave to have a sabbatical break away from the hall. From their home in Wellington New Zealand, they bravely answered an advertisement in the CCI (Christian Camping International) newsletter to come to Letton for a spell, and their time with us left many memories of their talents, their love and their enthusiasm. They gave so much of themselves during their first visit, and then returned in early 2001 for a shorter stay, with just as much flair and ability. Their keen and objective comments and stories have contributed much to this account.

Team members have continued to come and go, and will continue to do so until the workshop of the Lord has completed its work. Bill and Val Crudgington arrived in 2003, Richard and Rachel Kehoe in 2010, and Danny and Alison Pritchard in 2013. Neil and Jane Starling were appointed trustees in 2000, but surely the long-term-trustee award should go to John Currey.

In December 1981 (before he became a trustee), John wrote to me saying, "I'm sure the Lord is going to do great things at Letton ... My visit yesterday is having a great impact on me and is a further indication that God wants more of me! ... Margaret and I are now waiting on the Holy Spirit's guidance for our future ... we feel and hope that things will fit together for us/me to be involved as the financial man and assist in a practical way as well." More than thirty years of continuous and close involvement makes John and Margaret the longest serving members of Letton' s team, with the possible exception of Fergy the tractor! The Holy Spirit does indeed recruit well.

Some key members of the team - representatives of the
Adams, Carrolls, Roberts and Rootham families.

CHAPTER NINE

HOME LIFE

On Saturday 6th February 1982, Kay and I were married at Necton Parish Church in a ceremony conducted by the Rev Peter Taylor. Peter and Joy had been very supportive of Kay and me, and of Letton in general, and for several years it was the church we and visiting groups regarded as our home church. Before coming to Letton, Kay had been a member of two large churches in Norwich – Mount Zion and Holy Trinity – so a village church was very different, although lively and friendly.

Peter and Kay Carroll.

It had been just under two years since Mary had introduced me to Kay at the Norfolk and Norwich Hospital, where Kay had trained as a nurse. People say that those who have had one happy marriage often enter a second quite quickly when their partner dies, but the speed at which it all happened caught me by surprise. Just a month or two after Mary died, when thoughts of another relationship were completely out of my mind, I began to wonder if in fact it might be possible. But, I told myself, it certainly wouldn't be with a girl half my age, who in any case as a nurse was used to being objective in dealing with others. I was safe there!

But our relationship did develop and I was attracted by her spiritual insights and direct faith in God, particularly at a time when Letton was going through many growing pains. To these pains I added my own of behaving, rather embarrassingly, like a teenager in love, despite being in my early forties.

We were surrounded by advice from all sides, including from friends who had entered second marriages themselves and who pointed out that a second marriage is not simply a continuation of the first, so we needed to be sure. We decided that it would be a good thing to spend some time apart and Kay took up a nursing job in South Africa for six months.

I found this period hard – as I guess I was supposed to! – and so I bombarded Kay with letters, including a proposal of marriage, and waited anxiously for her response. I kept a prayer journal at the time, which was almost completely dominated by our relationship, but on rereading it I can see I needed to arrive at a point of surrendering it fully to God before he allowed a response. When that response arrived, shortly afterwards, it came in the form of three separate items from Kay, written at different times but linked up somewhere in the postal system. I didn't really care how it had happened, but was just delighted and relieved to have an answer in triplicate. I felt I had been loved back to life.

Married life at Letton was not very straightforward. The trustees and team had taken on board the aims of Haggai 2:9 ("The glory of this present house will be greater than the glory of the former house"), and as a family we had adopted the benchmark of Haggai 1:4: "Is it a time for you yourselves to be living in your panelled houses, while this house remains a ruin?"

Kay watering the flowers.

In practice, this meant we evaluated every project that needed doing in the family accommodation against the priorities of the rest of the property, to make sure we didn't get the work out of balance. For Kay and me, it meant returning from honeymoon to a very basic flat, with the kitchen sink literally propped up on boxes. Kay set about homemaking with determination and a natural skill, which was and still is one of her great gifts. One of the things we had lost when Mary died was a home base, but we hadn't realised it until Charlie the dog made us aware. We had rescued Charlie from an RSPCA home and he was a lively and lovable dog – but he couldn't settle at Letton. He needed a family fireside and a 'home', and was restless and unsettled without one. When some friends took him back to their own home he settled in and was once again the happy dog we used to know. At Letton, our family flat had become reduced to just a collection of rooms as an extension to the main hall, and we were unsettled without fully realising it. Kay set about making it a home once more.

My son Simon was living at Letton at this time, and took on improvements to the family flat as a gap-year project. One of the first things he tackled was the first floor kitchen, where the floor boards all sloped to the centre of the room. The cause was clear, because a large wooden beam underneath it had cracked. The obvious remedy was to jack up the beam and reinforce it with steel channel-sections on each side.

All was going well until someone outside the flat noticed that as Simon was jacking up the floor, the roof four metres above it was also going up. The internal walls had obviously been put in after the floor beam had collapsed. Once all the internal walls had been demolished, the floor could be more or less levelled. Easy, once the problem had been identified! But nevertheless, any spilt liquid on the kitchen still ran into the centre of the floor, although the slope was not so obvious.

Happily, other jobs were more straightforward. We had brought a dishwasher with us from Sussex but Kay felt that this was really rather an indulgent appliance to have in the kitchen, so had declined to use it. But when she was in hospital giving birth to Jenny, Simon and I installed it on the pretext of male needs, and we've had one in our kitchen ever since.

Kay's role coming into Letton was a difficult one. First of all, she had to be step-mum to three children who were not much younger than she was and, moreover, to three teenagers who had just lost their own mother at a very needy time in their lives. When our own three children arrived, life only got busier and more demanding, and when the pressures of Letton were added to all this it's clear what an amazing job she carried out. When money was tight, and Letton's finances were stretched to the limit, Kay worked several night shifts each week as a nurse in order to put food on the family table. It is no exaggeration to say that Letton Hall would not have survived without her.

Someone who visited us in our family, but also saw us in our Letton context, said, "Kay comes across as an exceptional person with a lot to give ... and I can't think of a more charming and gracious hostess for Letton than dear Kay." This is all the more interesting, knowing how differently Kay and I responded to our visitors. From the vantage point of our first-floor kitchen we could see groups as they arrived and, whereas I would drop everything and rush down to greet the people with enthusiasm, Kay would fight off a natural inclination to dive under the table and pretend she wasn't even there. By the same token, it meant of course that Kay *was* there for the *family*, whereas I just disappeared, leaving the family to wonder how important they were to me.

Kay and I came at things from a different point of view in many areas but we can only hope that our combined efforts made us a good team. I was happy standing up in front of a group of people and holding forth, whereas there are many testimonies from people who had been helped by Kay on an individual basis. And Kay certainly curbed some of my wilder schemes. I am reminded of the quote that "a pessimist is someone who has been compelled to live with an optimist" (Elbert Hubbard, *The Notebook*, 1929) and Kay has nobly borne her lot on a number of occasions.

As well as watching our visitors arrive, we could see other things too from our kitchen window vantage point, reminding us that we humans were far outnumbered by the wildlife around us. Mice were an everyday feature of life and provided entertainment during dinner parties in the kitchen, and birds nested noisily in the chimney, falling down the chimney with a great flapping of sooty wings every so often. Rats did not show themselves very frequently, but we knew they were there and of course, when Dolphin Court had been the stables, food would have been plentiful, so we were not too surprised when it took the humans a few years to claim that habitat back from them! There was a kind of uneasy truce with the rats as humans arrived in greater numbers.

Most evenings around dusk we could see bats flitting around the buildings, but it was only when they decided to come indoors that they caused us any problems. And when one would occasionally decide to cling to the bedroom wall of a visitor who wasn't used to country living, the problems approached panic levels. With their keen hearing, bats are not very easy to catch. They would happily allow someone armed with a rolled up newspaper or jam-jar to get very close, only to fly off just as capture or sudden death seemed within reach, and cling tantalisingly close on a nearby wall.

They occasionally visited Phil and Pat Webb at bedtime in the North Wing, and Phil entertained us with stories of how Pat would retire, completely hidden under the duvet, while Phil had to leap around the bedroom in his night-attire chasing a visiting bat. They decided after some time that the best way to deal with the problem was to leave the window open a little, go to bed trying to forget their uninvited visitor – and pray. The power of prayer seemed to show itself in all sorts of ways!

Pheasants were another feature of life at Letton; pretty to look at, but with some kind of inbuilt death-wish. They even allowed themselves to be caught by our small cat, who would then proudly drag them upstairs as a present for us, straddling a bird three times his own size between his legs. As each shooting season drew to a close, the number of pheasants around Letton's grounds increased. We held the shooting rights over our land and did not permit the shoot to visit, so as a general rule the pheasants, feeling relatively safe, took refuge with us as other areas were cleared. However, once or twice a year we allowed the shoot to come to Letton. On a couple of occasions we became quite closely involved, once when our large living room window was shattered by a fleeing bird, and once when a bird had been winged and flew straight through our bedroom window and landed beside the bed on Kay's side. The shooter happened to be the leader of the shoot, who had to put up with a considerable amount of banter about how he'd landed a bird at the bedside of the Lady of the Manor.

Our normal (and traditional) reward for allowing the shoot to use our land was a brace of pheasants hung on our door knob at the end of the day. At first, this was quite a novelty and Simon even managed to pluck and gut them one year. But this really didn't seem to be worth the time, trouble and mess it caused, with feathers and innards everywhere. The next stage we went through was to hang the pheasants for an appropriate time (although we were never quite sure how long this should be) and then take them to the local butcher, who would prepare them for us. However, this system also came to an end when the butcher tactfully suggested that hanging them was fine, but could we please not leave them until they were in an advanced stage of decay. The final and very welcome arrangement was for us to be invited to collect a brace from the butcher's freezer, fully oven-ready, neatly wrapped in cling film. Kay feared her facial expressions of hidden horror had helped to speed up this solution.

Since our kitchen looked out over the rather blank wall of Dolphin Court, we thought it might be attractive to have a wall-mounted dovecote there, suitably inscribed with Matthew 3:16. We imported some white doves from friends in Necton and for a while we enjoyed the sight of them flying around – but cats, rats and crows enjoyed having them around too. We also tried some fan-tailed doves, but as their main weapon of defence seemed to be to stand still and puff out their chest, this didn't prove very effective in the face of cars arriving in the turning-circle, so these too did not survive. We wondered about keeping peacocks, but were deterred by terrible tales of how much noise they made.

Family life at Letton was full of enjoyment and fascination with the wildlife around us, but we had to accept that we were really only there to serve the Lord in his workshop, so had to focus on our human visitors. It was sometimes quite difficult, as escaped sheep and runaway pigs running round our grounds were impossible to ignore – but we had to keep trying!

Kay on the dry rot hunt, between floors.

CHAPTER TEN

MAKING THE TEA

In my engineering apprenticeship I realised that as an apprentice, I shouldn't expect career highlights and recognition, although making tea for everyone was usually well received. But there were also moments when entertainment was provided at the expense of apprentices. For instance, sending them to the engineering stores for "a tin of elbow grease" or "a long weight" usually provided a laugh, especially if it could be done in front of a large crowd of other people in the factory.

It was recognised that the training of engineering apprentices was necessary, because jobs often did need more than the one pair of craftsman's hands; but most important of all, it was necessary to teach teamwork and to show that there were often boring and run-of-the-mill jobs that needed to be done to achieve an overall result. How true this was (and is) in the Lord's workshop – and how hard it was to learn the lesson sometimes.

One Sunday morning, I looked out of my bedroom window and saw that the lawn below was littered with piles of yellowy paper, and that the ground appeared to be wet. With a sinking heart I realised what it meant. The drains were blocked somewhere and the outflow from toilets high up in the house were causing the drain covers to lift off, with sewage bubbling out everywhere. I knew what I had to do, and I wasn't looking forward to it.

As I worked away with drain-rods to unblock the drain and, clad in overalls, wellington boots and rubber gloves, started to rake and brush up the foul-smelling deposits from the grass, I conducted a blunt and direct exchange with the Lord. "Look, I've got an honours degree in Engineering Science from a top university, I'm a Professional Engineer, I'm an ex-Managing Director and Management Consultant, I've got better things to do with all that training, and I'm not even getting paid to do this ... is this really all you've got to offer me Lord?!"

No answer. Until, that is, the leader of the group staying with us came to look for me once I'd cleaned myself up. He said, "We've had the most wonderful time this morning. We felt the Spirit of the Lord with us like we've never felt before. We've been praying for years for this in our church, and now it's all happening. Thank you!"

There is a verse in Psalms (84:10) where the psalmist says he'd "rather be a doorkeeper in the house of the Lord ..." A lesson I had to keep on learning.

One evening, on another occasion, I had just finished doing some work in Dolphin Court, which was intended to ensure that the water supply to the main hall was running freely. We were having a problem and I hoped I had fixed it before the water in the kitchens and toilets ran out and brought about all sorts of panic. As I walked across towards the hall in the gathering dusk, I saw three figures walking – or rather marching – towards me, silhouetted against the background of the hall. We had a large group of Girls' Brigade members staying with us, and the sight of three of their uniformed leaders striding out shoulder to shoulder towards me filled me with dread. It must be the water … it's stopped … how I can explain it …what can I say? We met in an open area of gravel for what I feared was going to be a shoot-out in the moonlight. My heart sank.

"We just wanted to tell you," they said, "that more than thirty of our girls made a commitment to become Christians tonight."

It didn't seem too bad then, to be an apprentice in the Lord's workshop, when he was doing that sort of work. A lot of our problems seemed to be linked with our water supply. So much so, that it warrants a chapter to itself later. In winter, the water tower would sometimes freeze up and there would be no water available on tap anywhere in the property. It's interesting how quickly civilised life degenerates into something quite primitive when that happens. Two days without water was the normal limit, even for accustomed and well-prepared residents, and of course, it was quite impossible to have groups staying with us if there was no water.

Norwich Youth For Christ leaders were due to stay one weekend and we had been working day and night trying to unfreeze the water tower. The top of the tower was encased with ice and ten-foot icicles were hanging down all round, but we knew that if we could free up the outlets from the underside of the tower, at least we would not have to cancel the group. It involved working for hours with frozen wet hands, undoing heavy bolts and disconnecting lengths of unyielding steel and plastic pipe in order to apply heat by lighting fires and using gas torches – and doing all this in the dark, soaked to the skin.

We managed to get the water flowing just in time and I remember welcoming the group, standing in front of them in filthy wet overalls, not having washed or shaved for a couple of days. How could the Lord in his workshop make anything good out of this I wondered to myself. But when the group left a few days later, they were full of praise for all they had learnt together – and in particular, they said the way the sunlight shone through the ice at the top of the tower and broke off into many colours taught them a lot about their various gifts as leaders.

The Letton water tower, well frozen up.

Another area where I found myself challenged by the role of apprentice was to do with cars. At the time I ceased being a Managing Director, I had a Range Rover plus an 'executive limousine' and had also bought a two-year old open top MGB sports car for fresh air motoring. In addition, we brought to Letton a 1934 Rover Speed 14 Hastings Coupe and an Austin Ruby, both for eventual restoration. Quite a fleet, although it didn't seem too excessive at the time - but most of it had to go.

The Range Rover proved a really useful work horse for a couple of years around Letton, and was actually better at towing a trailer across muddy terrain than Fergy the tractor. But when we had to tow a six-berth Portaloo from London, and the fuel consumption dropped to nine miles per gallon, the Range Rover wrote its own death warrant.

At one point we were down to only the MG as a family car, for Kay and me and three young children. One challenging journey was to a wedding in the suburbs of London. I had rigged up seat belts on the parcel shelf behind the seats for the children, reinforcing the panel of the car with a length of steel from an old mowing machine, but it wasn't to present day standards of child seats by any means. Anyway, we all squeezed in and headed off, with the two girls strapped in the back and young Ben slung in front of Kay, anticipating easy parking and a place to change into our smart clothes when we arrived, perhaps in the church hall or somewhere similar - but there was nothing of the kind. It was a city church surrounded by yellow lines and busy traffic.

We had to park on a nearby road where the houses opened up straight onto the pavement. We knocked on the door of the house we had parked outside and explained our predicament. To our great relief, they entered into the spirit of the adventure and watched in amazement as five sweaty and travel stained bodies emerged from the tiny car and went into their front room to change into wedding gear. But the MG wasn't going to cope for long as the children grew up, even for a committed apprentice. A family car was an absolute essential at Letton and we felt justified in setting out a shopping list in front of the Lord, even though we had no idea at all how it might be met. But the Lord was clearly determined to equip the workshop.

Some Christian friends were replacing their car and offered us their old one at a very helpful price, but it was still way outside our budget. It ticked all the boxes on our list, and as a bonus it was an attractive shade of red, but it was still too expensive. Then it came to our mind that we had a high wall built of Norfolk red bricks (Letton's old Melon House) that needed to be demolished for safety reasons, and we also had a team of people from a government Manpower Services scheme who at that time had nothing earmarked on their programme. The sale of the bricks almost completely paid for the car, with the rest coming from sale of a giant bath that was too big to use and far too expensive ever to fill!

Life at Letton was very much 24/7, and we welcomed any chance of a break that came along. On one occasion, we were staying for a few days at Ken and Pat Webb's caravan in Derbyshire when we received a message from the site office: "Could we please phone Letton as a matter of urgency." We received this news rather ungraciously, muttering about how we couldn't even get away for a couple of days without being bothered – but we complied, only to receive a rather cryptic instruction to phone another number. This turned out to be an elder of a local Gospel Hall, who said they had recently sold their property and wished to make us a personal gift as full-time Christian workers - and thought we might like to know as soon as possible over the phone before receiving written confirmation. Humble pie was on the menu that evening!

We decided quite quickly what we wanted to do with the gift and called in at the Denby Pottery works on our way back home the following day, convincing ourselves that the minor diversion we had to make meant it was really on the way. There was a factory sale on at the time, and also racks and racks of "seconds" in the design and colour we liked, and we indulged ourselves by choosing a complete twelve-piece set of practically everything. We were hugging each other with delight as we drove back to Letton, but at the same time feeling rather worried. "Had we overdone it? When were we ever going to use twelve sets of *anything*? Had we *over*-indulged?"

As we drove up to our flat, there were some cars outside and we realised we had unexpected guests. This wasn't at all unusual, because people often felt they could drop in to Letton and it was part of our role to welcome and entertain them. But this time, the timing was significant. Before we had even got our suitcases out of the car we had unpacked the Denby and exactly twelve cups, saucers and tea plates had been proudly washed, set out, and were fully in use. The Lord had endorsed the generosity of His servants in that Brethren Hall!

In my engineering apprentice days there was a saying doing the rounds: "We the unwilling, led by the unknowing, are doing the impossible for the ungrateful. We have done so much for so long with so little we are now qualified to do anything with nothing." (Konstantin Jurecek, the Czech diplomat and historian, 1854-1918. The quotation is occasionally attributed to Mother Theresa, but it's not really her attitude at all.)

Sometimes, life as an apprentice in industry seemed like that. But how different for the apprentice in the Lord's workshop. When the Master takes note of your needs and supplies them, then thanks and praise can know no bounds.

CHAPTER ELEVEN

THE LORD AT WORK

The main work of the Lord in his workshop at Letton was with the visitors who came - in groups of usually between twenty-five and one hundred, more than one hundred groups every year, so around four to five thousand people annually. That's a lot of opportunities for God to be at work!

*A group worshipping together and enjoying
fellowship on the back lawn.*

Serving as apprentices, we were often in the background, so although we may have been experiencing the work of the Lord in our own lives, we only caught occasional glimpses of the Master's work with the visitors. Group leaders, of course, told us of their highlights, often with tears of joy in their eyes.

It seemed that when people put aside time away for the Lord, he responded by pouring out blessings. Groups who had been meeting together in their home environment for years without much obvious result, suddenly found that at Letton the floodgates opened. For our part, we became so accustomed to amazing things happening that it was difficult not to become over-familiar with seeing the power of God at work.

This changed when we were running our own programmes and were able to see the Lord's activities at first hand, but since we prayed for all groups visiting Letton, we were constantly on the lookout for answered prayer.

VISITORS BOOKS

One source of information of what God was doing came in what people put in the visitors book, which each group was invited to fill in with their comments. The results were varied! Sometimes, there was nothing but insider-jokes and pages of nearly illegible scrawl, despite our warning inside the front of each book to "Ponder carefully what you write. At least three thousand other people will read it each year, and what's worse, if you write something embarrassing, *you* will have to read it when you visit again!"

But throughout the pages, there were also some thoughtful comments, sometimes with drawings or poems, some insights shared, and some deeply personal words that helped to give a flavour of the work the Lord was doing in people's lives. Groups included people of different ages and cultural backgrounds, and from different countries in some cases, each with different reasons for coming to Letton. Some came for Christian purposes, but some for other purposes, such as school or training visits. The attributions beside each quotation illustrated this wide range, and all contributed to provide a kind of mosaic of experiences of life at Letton.

What follows is a selection of comments made by visitors across the years, but it is only a small selection, and from an incomplete mosaic at that. In total, there are twenty-two visitors books covering the period of this account, and many more subsequently, and it is only possible to include a tiny fraction of comments. Therefore, those I have included here must serve to give an impression of what was going on.

The presence of the Lord

Wonderful house, wonderful atmosphere – the Lord is here. Letton Hall is beautiful – full of God's presence – very peaceful. (A Norfolk church group)

Great! This really is a House for the Lord. (A Navigators work party)

Surely the Lord is in this place. (A Kart Camp member)

God was here and we met Him. (A local church house party)

I really felt the Holy Spirit here. (A member of a training course)

An amazing God and a great place to enjoy to Him. (A visiting church from Cambridgeshire)

About the people working at Letton – the apprentices

Thank God for your vision – it has enlarged ours. (An evangelical youth group)

Letton Hall defines the gift of hospitality. Thanks for serving us. (A USAF chaplain)

We had a wonderful, great, inspiring, tremendous and really blessed time at Letton Hall. Thank you for your care, kindness and hospitality. (A German student)

Thanks for your service and ministry to us, providing us with this lovely place. (A Cambridge church)

Thanks for the welcome and the hospitality – it made us feel wanted. (A university Christian Union)

The Lord has certainly blessed Letton and its staff. Thanks to them and Him. (A Kart Camp member)

Thank you God for giving your vision to people who have put it into action. (An Essex church)

The most welcoming house I've ever been to. (A member of a young peoples' house party)

Continue to let Jesus shine through you all. We have been truly blessed. (A missionary fellowship)

Personal Testimony

A lost soul now found – please remember me. (A student from a College of Art and Technology)

Now I am a Christian. (A member of a Letton Family Week)

I was healed by Jesus – I can't thank you enough. (A member of a community church)

I came here and found peace – God gave me a big hug. (A member of a Norfolk parish church)

God can change your life. (A young people's house party member)

I was filled with the Holy Spirit today ... and from another person ... *Best day of my life.* (Both from a Norfolk church group)

God spoke to us here. Thank you. (A member of a Peterborough church)

I have become a Christian and I now feel complete and happy. He has made a whole new horizon for me and none of that would have been possible unless I came to Letton Hall. I am truly grateful! (A member of a young people's group)

Work Parties

I thought Nehemiah had problems until I came here! (A member of a Navigators work party

Hope we've made a big enough impression – if not we'll come again next year. (Another member of the same work party)

The Letton vision for preserving and developing something good is much appreciated. (A visitor)

Timetable: Devotions 6.30am: Project Planning 7.30am ... (From the programme of a committed USAF work Party erecting a staircase in Dolphin Court)

The rugged old building, Oh it is a sight; With a lot of love and prayer, I'm sure we can put it right. The walls are crumbling, windows are dropping, one has a crooked fire door; But God thinks, what a lovely place. A lovely sacred place, I'm sure. (An Essex community church)

Romance!

To Adrian. My love is like a cabbage, divided into two. My leaves I give to others, my heart I save for you. (An irresistible message from a young peoples' house party!)

Bo Yeon is a pretty girl. I like her. (From a Korean church group)

My boyfriend became a Christian. (From a Family Week team member)

At my first Letton visit I met ----- . I am now at my last Letton, engaged to this lovely man ... and I have only Letton to blame! (From one of the regular youth group visitors to Letton)

A vocation found?

Great kitchens – found my vocation in life. Had a great time! (A university CU member)

I really enjoyed my stay at Letton Hall, even the washing up! (A member of an evangelistic fellowship)

93

... And some generally encouraging comments

God is great. (An Essex Gospel Hall)

Things only change for the good at Letton. (A Norfolk parish church)

Truly a blessing. (A Croydon church)

Thanks to the Lord and Letton Hall. We enjoyed every moment of our stay. (A Cambridgeshire Baptist church)

There's something or Someone about this place that makes us want to keep on coming back! (An Essex church)

Good ol' Letton. Wonderful as always. (A youth group member)

A lovely house with Spirit. Every weekend is a winner. (A Norwich church)

Thanks for the time of my life. (A member of a visiting school group)

The visitors book comments above are from groups where we were more-or-less in the background, sometimes providing a full catering service but often just answering queries, solving problems, and of course, running Go-Kart sessions. It isn't clear from the above quotations, but the most common topic on every page of the visitors books was Go-Karting. Much as we might have hoped for deep spiritual insights, we had to content ourselves with enthusiastic karting comments – and since Go-Karting had been an element in the vision for Letton as it developed, we had to accept that it was part of the Lord's plan.

Certainly, it attracted all ages from the under-fives to the over eighties, both men and women, and from bishops to "bad lads," providing challenge and excitement, even pain and injury at times – and soaking wet clothes whenever it rained. (The karts were fitted with bucket seats, and buckets naturally filled when conditions were wet.) But karting very often provided highlights for visiting groups in many ways, and it became important to maintain the facility. Entertainment, fun, and the thrills of competition were (and are) very much part of the Letton experience.

FAMILY WEEKS

We were much more directly involved in some of the activities at Letton, one of the main ones being Family Weeks. These started through a number of circumstances, coinciding in a pattern which we came to recognise as the Lord putting His agenda into practice.

First of all, we found that from time to time we had some key summer weeks available at short notice and it seemed a waste of our resources not to do something about it. There was a family feel about Letton, so that seemed a natural avenue to explore. Also, we had had some contact with CLASP (The Christian Link Association of Single Parents), who had run an activity themselves at Letton, and although we did not set out initially to concentrate on single-parent holidays, we realised that several of the Letton team had personal experience of single parenting themselves. Over a year or two, the pattern established itself and Letton's value-for-money Family Weeks became predominantly for single parents.

A Family Week group photo.

A Family Week young leaders team.

An information sheet for one particular year included these aspects:

- *FAMILY: The emphasis will be on "family," with activities for all ages, both together and with times for parents and children to "do their own thing" apart. Absence makes the heart grow fonder we're told.*
- *FUN: There'll be lots for everyone! We'll be arranging visits to local holiday attractions including seaside, forests, the Norfolk Broads and fine Norwich City. We'll also be having a number of activities based at Letton – and if your idea of fun is relaxing and unwinding there'll be time for that too.*
- *FRIENDSHIP: Many people who have come on Family Weeks in the past have become firm friends, sometimes discovering things in common that they can share together. So, come to meet new friends ... or introduce one of your present circle of friends to Letton.*
- *FELLOWSHIP: Underpinning the concept of Family Weeks here is our experience of seeing God bless time spent away together in a Christian environment. Spiritual batteries are recharged and it's no exaggeration to say that lives have changed dramatically through meeting God in new ways.*
- *FOOD: Plenty of good home cooking to add to the enjoyment of it all. Plus an easily digestible diet of spiritual food, too.*

To meet this programme the resident team at Letton had to make sure we had someone to lead teaching sessions and to lead the worship, either from ourselves or from outside and, most important of all, to recruit a young peoples' team of responsible youngsters from local churches and families. These young people were a vital part of the programme, injecting energy and enthusiasm into the proceedings, looking after the visiting children, and in the course of this, developing friendships amongst themselves that have lasted for many years.

Looking back, one of my lasting impressions from several Family Weeks is of greeting new arrivals at Letton's front door.

Very often this would be a parent – a mother usually, but occasionally we had single fathers - walking up the steps rather apprehensively, with children sticking very close, not at all sure what to expect. They might be used to being highly dependent on each other all the time, close, never very far away from one another, accustomed to sticking together for mutual support. Yet here they were being greeted by both an adult and a member of the young peoples' team, with an invitation to do separate things once they had found their room and settled in. A look of panic sometimes crossed the parent's face – it was obvious that this didn't feel at all comfortable for them.

The children usually made themselves at home first, with one of the young leaders introducing them to other children who all seemed happy and relaxed, ready to kick a ball round together, or explore this big new house that seemed so exciting. It was not unusual, an hour or two later, to find the parent looking rather puzzled, wondering how, for the first time in years, their children didn't seem to need them around for every moment. But it didn't take them long to realise that this gave them freedom to meet and chat to other parents in exactly the same situation.

A really important aspect of each Family Week was to have a time each morning, and most evenings, during which adults could enjoy fellowship and teaching, and have a chance to share their experiences together. As with the young leaders, this often resulted in long-lasting friendships. The comments made by Family Week guests could fill many pages here, but just one will have to suffice. It was made by a visitor who had been to several weeks, and her few words cover a lot:

> *"It has been such a wonderful week and God has done great things. Thanks to all the team for making it special."*

Two more Family week memories are recounted in Appendix 18 (p.182).

THE PARABLE OF THE MIRY PIT

There was a certain man who went on a journey, to seek out the spring of the water of life. And many people journeyed with him, and they talked with one another along the way, and great was their rejoicing.

But verily, the road was hard and narrow was the way, and the people cried out "Forsooth, veer not to the right, neither to the left, O Simon son of Gerald... but keepest thou to the solid ground, that we mightest each our journey's end and that our joy might be complete."

But Simon, son of Gerald heard not their cries, neither heeded their words of wisdom. Instead he hearkened unto the foolish words of Jonathan of Kingston-upon-Thames and other false prophets who counselled him to take the broad and easy way that leadeth to destruction.

And the people said "Is this Jehu, son of Nimshi, for lo. he driveth furiously".

And it came to pass as they journeyed, that they did sink into a deep and miry pit, and there was weeping and gnashing of teeth.

And the people said, "Lo, thou shalt no longer be called Simon, son of Gerald, but Michael, son of Schumacker"....

And it was so.

This extract from the Visitors' Book tells the story of a Family Week expedition through the woods in Fergy's trailer when Simon Rootham got the tractor stuck in the mud and the trip had to be abandoned.

GERMAN STUDENT WEEKS

Letton was discovered by a number of German Christian student groups a few years after we opened, and from that time onwards our summer season always included at least two weeks, and sometimes up to four or five weeks, of visitors from Germany. The pattern of each visit was usually similar, with a coach-load of young people, complete with food and special kit, being dropped for between ten days and a fortnight outside Letton's front door.

The situation only became more complicated when there was an outgoing group to be taken back to Germany on the same coach. This put quite a load on our logistics, with one group packed up and ready, leaving by the back door while the incoming group came in through the front and were entertained in the library with welcome chats etc for as long as possible to give time for essential housekeeping tasks to be carried out, before they could take possession of the house.

I sometimes wondered whether the groups of German young people felt rather abandoned as their familiar coach disappeared down the drive and they were deposited in the depths of rural Norfolk. What were they going to do? Where were the English tourist attractions they no doubt hoped to visit? And how would they get there anyway, surrounded as they were by fields and with no transport at hand?

But this very isolation seemed to produce a special type of house party. They made themselves at home, with their own cooks providing familiar (and delicious!) food, and all the notices and signs around the house changed into German overnight. They were generally among the most creative of all our visitors, both in the activities they planned and in the craftwork and decorations that began to appear around Letton. Of course, they also enjoyed the Go-Karts, and we did the best we could to provide driving tuition and safety rules in German.

One particular leader decided he wanted to provide a more ambitious way of experiencing the English environment by taking his group on a two-day cycle to the North Norfolk coast. We worked with him in planning the adventure and were able to obtain use of a church hall in Cromer for basic overnight accommodation. But provision of bicycles presented more of a problem. We scraped together enough for the pilot scheme, but for the following year we decided we had to do better.

We came across an advert in a motoring magazine for a quantity of brand new Russian bicycles, offered at half the price we could buy elsewhere, so decided to investigate. Apparently they had been accepted by a car dealer in Yorkshire (hence the ad in a motoring journal), in lieu of payment for a car he had sold, and he assured us they were still crated up and ready for simple reassembly – so we ordered thirty.

We awaited their arrival with some excitement and they duly arrived, certainly looking the part. They were finished in a metallic khaki colour and decorated with red stars. They had an obvious Russian look about them, but we felt that didn't really matter, since in all other ways they appeared to be serviceable new bikes. Full instructions were provided, happily with pictures so we didn't need to translate fully from the Russian.

Our first misgivings came when some of the nuts seemed not to tighten fully when we were assembling the bikes, and we realised that we were stripping the threads because of the poor quality of the metal. Gradually, we came to realise that poor quality materials had been used throughout, but came to the conclusion that if we knew the weak spots and adjusted them carefully, then the bikes were serviceable. But that didn't stop us fitting out the Letton trailer with racks for half-a-dozen bikes as a precaution, so that we could respond to emergency calls from anywhere around Norfolk.

We aired our concern in that issue of Letton News:

Imagine the scene ... in early summer a well-drilled squad of foreign-speaking nationals fanned out towards strategic towns in Norfolk passing close by the high security Royal Residence of Sandringham. They were mounted on military style cycles painted Khaki with red star markings, and the leaders carried printed booklets in Russian containing mysterious diagrams. Was it all as sinister as it looked?

Well, of course it wasn't, and the only incidents reported concerned our cyclists, puzzled by some of Norfolk's enigmatic road signs, having to ask the way. It was all generally regarded as a success; so much so, that we decided to establish a fleet of bikes to be available for all our groups, although not relying on Russian machines in the future. This scheme lasted for quite a few years, but eventually the time and trouble required from an already hard-pressed team to keep the bikes in good order led to a slow decline. (Incidentally the same fate awaited the Scalextric car track set out in the basement.)

The Russian bikes.

The German groups seemed to attract dramatic situations. One group suffered a significant problem on each of the ten days of their visit, ranging from police attention in Great Yarmouth to a suspected painkiller overdose needing a dash to the A and E Department of the Norfolk and Norwich Hospital. Another girl suffered some kind of fainting attack and remained completely unconscious for quite some time, until the ambulance arrived.

Those incidents alone kept them high on Letton's daily prayer list, but the most serious involved a girl who went on a planned theatre trip to London to see *Blood Brothers*, but didn't get on the bus to return. Apparently the theatre production had triggered really painful memories of her own family situation, so instead of returning north to Norfolk she continued on south back to Germany. All was well once she made contact and let people know what she had done, but it was desperately worrying until that happened.

A young girl with another group developed a health problem that apparently could only be treated by her consultant in Switzerland – and she needed treatment urgently. Around midday we started investigating options and to our satisfaction (and with the knowledge that finances were not to be a limiting factor), we were able to get her and a companion to Zurich that evening, while her companion made it back to Letton for a late breakfast the following morning. It made us realise that Norfolk was not quite as cut off as we sometimes felt, and it increased our fellowship with our continental visitors.

THE GO-KART CAMPS

The West Runton Dolphin Camp organisation had been extremely helpful and supportive in establishing Letton in the early days, and the organisation was very keen to reap the benefit as soon as possible. A Kart Camp was in fact our first fee-paying visiting group as opposed to work parties, and arrived while the concrete of the kart track was barely cured. Conditions were very basic, but it was a relief for the camp to feel that once it had arrived it could store all its equipment and not have to pack it up and take it away afterwards. Moreover, long term plans could be set in motion for future use of the track and of Dolphin Court generally. (Incidentally, we had thought at an early stage that it would be good to name the stables "Dolphin Court" in recognition of the help the West Runton organisation had given us.)

(Above) One of the first trips out on the new kart track.
(Below) Kart Camp in action.

The camp was committed to using tents for sleeping accommodation, as this was seen to add a constructive element to the activity. The tents were stored at Letton, so this was no problem, and also foam mattresses were bought. But in the early stages we learned of what threatened to be an insurmountable problem. Our Local Authority had been very supportive from the outset and had even classed us as "a Conference Centre under construction," which apart from being true, also reduced the Council Tax we had to pay. They had also given us planning permission, which included a Go-Kart track and tents and a few caravans for a limited time each year.

The problem arose, because it was suddenly realised that we now had to comply with the specific requirements for a campsite. The Local Authority only notified us of this at short notice, with just a few weeks to go before a Kart Camp was due to arrive. We could comply with most things, such as fire points and means of audible warning, but an official campsite also needed a special type of stainless steel deep sink to be installed and plumbed in. This presented a serious problem, because of both the time and money constraints. To acquire a special design before the camp arrived was practically impossible, and we faced the situation of the camp arriving only to be told they had nowhere to sleep because they couldn't use tents.

The need was known by everyone living and working at Letton at that time, including Tim Baldwin who had come up from London for the weekend. Tim had to return on Sunday evening, but phoned when he'd arrived home with rather an odd message: "You know you need a sink unit? Well, as I drove down the A14, I noticed what looked like a sink unit that had obviously been dumped by the roadside near the junction with the A11. I didn't stop to look at it. It's probably nothing like what you need but you might like to check it out."

We did indeed check it out that Monday morning, just in case. We drove down to the spot with the Range Rover and trailer and, to our amazement, found that it looked very much like what we needed. On return to Letton, we found it was in good condition and to precisely the right specification for a camp site. One team member said rather ungratefully (and facetiously), "but it hasn't got a plug attached to the chain." However, our general reaction was to give praise to God and realise that He really did intend Kart Camp to happen!

One of the first Kart Camps in residence at Dolphin Court.

These kart camps flourished and grew as the years went by and of course, the track and karts were used and enjoyed by practically every other visitor to Letton. As their use increased, so did the shortcomings of the original rough concrete track surface. Karts, and any electronic devices attached to them, were rattling to pieces and it was decided that the track needed resurfacing.

The original layout of the track had stood the test of time, but it was also agreed that it should be widened in a couple of places. The story of the finances for this is told elsewhere, but gradually the track facility was improved, and it is good to record that it all started from the original Kart Camp set-up.

The karts themselves also developed. The Kart Camps – now up to four or five per year – bought faster and noisier karts, causing the Local Authority to measure the level of sound and conclude that we were guilty of sound pollution. In response to this, we tried out nearly silent electric karts, but rejected them as difficult to re-charge under Letton conditions, as well as being expensive. Eventually a solution was reached by limiting the hours of karting, which although inconvenient for the Kart Camps, did pacify the neighbour who was most affected. Also, the camps were encouraged to develop activities other than karting, which widened their appeal for some youngsters.

Letton gradually increased the size of their fleet, buying karts that were robust enough to stand up to the use and abuse they received; and for an interesting few months we also benefitted from the services of a volunteer who had his own kart production unit in Thetford. Terry Fullerton was held by Ayrton Senna to be the best kart driver he had ever raced against, so Letton can boast of serious racing connections, as well as providing fun for all visitors

All was not easy or enjoyable, however, and a tragedy occurred at an early Kart Camp when sixteen-year-old Mark Bushell was electrocuted while taking a shower. The problem was due to a mains electricity cut-out switch not operating correctly, despite having been checked just six days previously by the electricity board. The coroner ruled that we were in no way responsible, but despite that, the incident left us all very sad and full of regret.

Mark's family presented the camp with a silver trophy cup in his memory, to be competed for each year, and in a letter said: "Let us hope that in time, some purpose for all this will be found." For our part, that purpose was to remind us of our responsibilities under God.

MID-WEEKS OF MOTORING FUN

The Care For The Family charity instituted a programme of holidays entitled 'Adventures in Parenting' with the aim of providing opportunities for a parent to spend time away with one of their children in a Christian environment, to develop better relationships. "Building memories that last," was the slogan adopted and Letton was invited to participate. Our programme was mainly directed towards fathers and sons, although the occasional mother and daughter were welcomed if they wished to apply. (Incidentally, we did arrange a successful one-off 'Mothers and Daughters Advent Break' but apparently, mothers and daughters generally felt they couldn't be spared at home just before Christmas and this experiment wasn't repeated.)

A father and sons "Motoring Fun" group photo.

Our Go-Karting facility became the focus of each holiday but other items were added, all with a mechanical or motoring flavour. On various occasions, we sampled off-road driving, a few laps round Snetterton race track, visits to Letton by tanks or top-of-the-range cars, and father/son teams being given fast drives by our Rally-driving farmer neighbour. We also used parts of nearby Shipdham airfield for a series of driving activities, such as a father driving his car round a marked-out course with his son as a passenger - but with the father blindfolded and relying on his son's navigational instructions! Where insurance (and nerves) permitted, we also had sons driving their father's cars.

On the kart track, there was straightforward racing between father and son teams, or events such as 'Breakfast–in–Bed', where one leg of the race included the driver being served with a bowl of cereal, complete with milk and sugar, and having to finish it before the end of the lap. An egg obstacle race, with real raw eggs also caused amusement, as well as a lot of sticky mess around the track. In quieter moments, there were appropriate Christian sessions and activities where relationships could develop within each family unit as they spent more time together than normal – and perhaps more than they had ever done before.

I particularly remember one globe-trotting trouble-shooting accountant, who didn't normally have much time for or with his son. The lad was quite intelligent and able (playing cricket at county school level, for instance), but his father was forever running him down and not acknowledging his worth. It was quite painful to watch. On the last day, the boys were having a few farewell laps while some fathers looked on, when the lad in question had a nasty spill just outside the pits (after driving really well, otherwise). It looked as if he might have really hurt himself. Everything went suddenly quiet, as it often did after an accident, and then the father burst through the group of onlookers and rushed to his son's side and tended him caringly. The rest of us looked on quite moved.

There were many constructive moments during these father-son events. "Brilliant, Simply brilliant," was one son's comment. "Things we have heard and known, things our fathers have told us ... we will tell the next generation the praiseworthy deeds of the Lord" (Psalm 78:3-4).

SCHOOLS

School groups were always welcome at Letton Hall, not only because they helped to fill term time midweek periods when other groups were not able to use us, but also because they brought a freshness which made it a joy to share our house and facilities with them. Initially, our school group contacts came through teachers who had visited Letton personally as members of other groups but felt that Letton could be a suitable venue for school residentials, and together we learnt what was needed.

For schools from city-centre areas, just being in the country was enough of an adventure. For some youngsters, any area of green that was not a public park was something of a novelty, and to see farm animals at close quarters out in the fields was an unforgettable experience. Differentiating between pigs (= bacon) and cows (= beef burgers) was often entertaining, and to visit 'milk bottle fields' (pasture) or the 'bags-of-sugar fields' and pull up a sample of sugar beet (in conjunction with and permission from the local farm) was an absolute revelation.

It was also a revelation for many to experience living together as a group. Sitting down at a table for meals was a whole new concept for some, and the idea of sharing the chores of serving and clearing up required some persuasive teaching. But to us, being involved with education, even if only on the fringes, was quite a satisfying experience.

It didn't always go in a straightforward way of course, and one of our first 'moments' came after waving goodbye to the minibuses of a small school group, only to find them returning after less than an hour with the teachers asking us to watch the pupils leave the minibuses. Out they came, one by one, each one holding out a bag, which they proceeded to hand to us with downcast eyes and a rather ashamed look. Each bag was filled with household items they had 'liberated' from Dolphin Court – and it was a surprise to us to see just how much soap and how many toilet rolls they had managed to find. It was quite difficult not to smile but of course, fierce words had to be spoken.

At the opposite end of the scale were the independent schools who visited, often with some project in mind but almost always with a budget that could be spent on interesting activities. One of these involved visiting the local trout farm, hiring some fishing tackle and seeing what they could catch. "Far more than we ever thought possible," was the answer, and every freezer at Letton was commandeered to cope with the catch. Delicious barbecued trout was on the menu for the school group itself, and when that didn't make much of an inroad into the quantity of fish available, invitations were issued to everyone around to come for another barbeque. The private freezers of Letton's staff were filled and in theory, fish were also to be taken home to parents - but the transportation of melting fish was fraught with difficulty, so probably not much of it arrived. The main lesson learnt was not to underestimate the energy and determination of well-motivated young boys when equipped with a rod and tackle and well-filled fish ponds.

Enthusiastic young boys were always quick to take advantage of any opportunity, and did so when we organised a visit from the local police dog-handling base. The police used Dolphin Court regularly for training their dogs, because once guests had left we could offer the police a site full of human smells, and because of this the police were happy to provide occasional demonstrations in return.

When we arranged a visit for one school, it was decided that the police would give a demonstration of how a dog would chase after a fleeing villain and bring him down. The 'villain' would be protected by an arm band strapped to his arm. It had to be his *left* arm, the police officer stressed. A volunteer villain was called for and, of course, by the boys' popular vote, one of their masters was selected and the armband strapped on. And, naturally, the boys made sure the protection was on the *right* arm. There was obviously a lot of stage management involved, but the subsequent chase looked very realistic, and by the time it had been embellished by frequent retelling, it made a story that endured for years. The schoolmaster did survive, incidentally.

Several schools came so regularly that they became real friends. There was the Peterborough school that carried out a photographic and filming project each year, and the school from Surrey that took the Go-Karting very seriously and planned all sorts of competitions and driving activities with us, which increased in complexity each year.

One group, admittedly rather older than the normal school group since it was a School of Nursing and Midwifery, provided an interesting interlude. Their tutor had expressed the thought that it would be educational if they could know of any animals on the farm that would be giving birth during their stay. The farmer denied any pre-meditated malice, but a suitable cow started labour in the very early hours of one morning and the group was duly roused and trudged off to the cattle shed, blearily gathering round the pen. It was muddy and smelly and not an easy birth, so the sight of the herdsmen, at four o'clock in the morning, pulling on greasy and bloody ropes while a troubled mother-to-be protested loudly, may not have had quite the result the tutor had hoped for. Whatever the case, that particular request was never repeated in the future.

For more routine visits we produced work sheets that teachers could use to help their pupils gain more from the visit. These were designed to fit in with the current school curriculum and to encourage our visitors to use their powers of observation and imagination.

SPECIAL EVENTS

Letton was a workshop for the Lord but we were always mindful of the fact that it had originally been built with other aims in mind. It was designed as a family house with ample space and facilities for entertainment, leisure and pleasure, and 'business' had a very low profile in Sir John Soane's plans. One of my personal pleasures has always been to walk around the outside of the house at night, when all the rooms are lit up and people can be seen enjoying themselves inside - and I can imagine all the social occasions that have taken place at Letton down the centuries.

The Carroll family had been in residence for about eight years when Bridget's 21st birthday arrived and it didn't need much encouragement to think of an appropriately grand manner in which to celebrate this event. A Ball was planned, to be held on 3rd September 1988. Since that year also marked two hundred years since the completion of Letton Hall it was entitled the Bicentennial Ball. It was decided that approximately one hundred and fifty people could be accommodated, and it was to be a formal or period dress event.

To enhance the flavour of the period, guests were ushered into the hall by the back entrances so that they could go upstairs to a dressing room and make their formal entrance at the top of the staircase. They could then be announced by costumed flunkies (my son Simon and his fiancée Rachel) as they descended the stairs, to the accompaniment of minuets being played in the drawing room.

It was a memorable event and, despite being hard work, seemed to be enjoyed by the whole Letton team, it being good to re-enact something of the house's past; and since it was a Carroll family occasion, the modest shortfall of costs after ticket income was met by the family.

It was ten more years before the next ball was held, on 6th September 1997 and once again, the initiative came from the

Carroll family, who called it a Celebration Ball, on the rather flimsy pretext that a number of family birthdays added up to one hundred that year. It was rather more ambitious than the previous ball, with increased numbers allowed for, and with a marquee erected outside the garden door to help accommodate them. It was another memorable event, which this time covered its own costs.

A third ball came just two years later on 18th December 1999, billed as the Millennium Ball, with the aim of outshining all other millennium events and this time, as a "Roof-raising Ball," it was also aimed at fund-raising. Once again, it was more ambitious than the previous balls, with increased numbers and other attractions, such as an auction of promises. We raised approximately £2000 towards the cost of roof repairs, but also raised some problems when a group from London, who had won the bidding for a pig from the Letton herd, wondered how it would ride on the way back, strapped wriggling in the front seat!

Enjoyable though these balls were, they were very hard work for the resident team and inevitably led to questions as to whether they represented fair use of the resources of the Lord's workshop. Yet this was the same Lord who so obviously entered into social occasions enthusiastically during his time on earth, as the story of the wedding at Cana illustrates. Certainly, weddings were easier to accommodate and justify, and at the same time took advantage of Letton's natural role as a party venue.

One of the earliest wedding receptions we accommodated was for Bruce and Annie Eglington, who then became our neighbours at Garden Cottage, adjacent to the kart track. So, not only was it an enjoyable event but it also kept us in closer touch with our local community. Family weddings, and weddings linked with the Letton working team, helped to emphasise the feeling that Letton Hall was not a commercial venture but was really part of the Lord's family living and working together.

This same feeling of being a family was also reflected in the Victorian Family Fun Day in 1994, and also in more recent social and period events. It is hard not to be caught up with the attractions when living in a house originally planned for leisure and pleasure.

Chris Key and his new wife Jenny (nee Carroll) standing in the library beneath the Prayer Plaque, with Kay's brother Nick and his family.

The bride and groom arrive in a 1930 Humber Snipe, which had been rebuilt at Letton by the author over the preceding two years.

MEMORABLE MOMENTS

Letton Hall has provided a host of memorable moments over the years, but it is interesting that some of those that stick in the memory have nothing at all to do with Letton's role as a workshop of the Lord. It may be, of course, that it's just because they are so far removed from Letton's central purpose that they stand out, although some do perhaps give a clue to God's sense of humour.

For example, we received a fairly short notice enquiry for accommodation for a group of farmers coming from France to visit opposite numbers at an exchange function in Dereham. It was for just one night and the date was free, so we opened up negotiations with the local organiser. Most of it concerned time of arrival and parking for their coach, but we formed the clear impression that the group consisted of several young men, similar in age to the young local organiser, so we decided to keep the arrangements simple and straightforward from our point of view. We made up all the beds on the top floor of the hall which gave us more than enough numbers and also meant we could carry on with preparations for our next group of visitors in the rest of the hall

On the evening they were due to arrive, we waited to greet them – but there was no sign. We waited even longer, but still no sign. Eventually, we managed to contact someone in Dereham who knew a little about the exchange event, who said it was all going very well. So well, in fact, that the celebrations had taken on an alcoholic joviality that meant all track of time had been lost – so, could we wait up a little longer because they certainly were coming? Eventually the coach arrived and we watched in horror as the passengers stumbled out. They were certainly not all young, and some looked so old that we feared they would never manage the steep steps up to the bedrooms at the top of the hall. But what was even more concerning was that they were not all men. Several women were in the party too.

We attempted to explain our predicament, but what with language difficulties and the fact that by now it was well past midnight, they did not seem too concerned about details of the arrangements. We led them upstairs and they followed gamely behind, and when we reached the first bedroom, their leader ushered the first of them in line into it regardless of age or sex. And so it continued, until all the bedrooms were filled and all the visitors had been accommodated – and we went downstairs shaking our heads, wondering what on earth was going to happen after this mixed bag of sleeping arrangements! Next morning, they all appeared for breakfast, looking fit and well-rested, while we decided to say absolutely nothing at all! But we did at least resolve to find out a little more about our visitors in future.

Something similar occurred when a member of a visiting church group asked if we would consider accommodating a training course from his company. We recognised the name of the company as a major food supply company and, thinking that this might lead to a new area of business for us, we opened up negotiations.

Our first contact happened when a day or two before the group were due to arrive, a large white van pulled up outside the front door, looking as if it were so overloaded that its wheels were bowing outwards. The driver got out and puffed his way to the door looking as if he too was rather overloaded and asked where he should put it. "What is it?" we asked. "Well, it's the beer innit?" he said.

Having got over our initial shock, we finalised all the preparations and awaited the arrival of the group, which by now we had discovered was a course for East London pub landlords. Everything went well from our point of view, even the entertaining moment when we heard one of the cooks humming a Christian song in the kitchen. When we expressed a little curiosity he said, "Well, this *is* a Christian centre isn't it? I thought you wouldn't mind."

After the first visit the company made, we had a little difficulty wafting out the beery-pub smell from the drawing room in time for the Baptist Church who were coming in next - but for their second visit, we were a little more careful where we allowed the group to install the kegs of beer. Altogether, it was an entertaining interlude, and yet another example showing us that the work of the Lord's workshop was not limited to the Christian community. Hospitality was a key ingredient in our work, not just to the church but well beyond.

Then there was the time when the 'Joy riders' came, taking us even further into unfamiliar territory. We had been toying with the idea of setting up a pre-seventeen driving course, entitled Countdown, and had distributed some publicity brochures saying that there would be input on the course from the police on road safety matters. Somehow, the Norfolk Youth Justice Team heard of this and we began to explore a joint venture with them. It was aimed at dealing with joy riders – young people who stole cars simply for the joy of driving them around – which was a significant problem for the authorities. It was very difficult to communicate with the young people and modify their offending behaviour, even when they had done something really serious such as injure or kill someone on the roads.

The main parties involved were the Probation Service, the Social Services department, the Police and ourselves, and the idea was that by engaging in a popular activity like Go-Karting, we could open up communication and carry out some work on reducing their offending behaviour. It certainly opened up communication. It was fascinating to watch the course members bristle with hostility when their natural enemies the police turned up in a patrol car, only to see that reaction change after they'd been competing on equal terms on the kart track for a few laps. Suddenly, all inhibitions were dropped in their eagerness to compare lap times and cornering techniques. There was, of course, a lot of macho posturing, some of which was directed against their female probation officer.

"Come on Gill, why don't you have a go if you're not too scared." The result was fascinating to watch, as Gill proceeded to beat their lap times by a substantial margin. This was partly the result of her having been on a residential Kart Camp at Letton, wearing another hat, and had become an experienced Go-Kart driver – but however it had been won, respect was instantly achieved!

The local press caught wind of the activity and of course, the idea of teaching joy riders to drive faster made a good story and even inspired a large cartoon showing a car hurtling through the streets of Norwich on two wheels, scattering pedestrians in its wake. But I saw at first-hand, during seminar sessions after track time, how barriers came down and it was possible to address the key issues. It was impossible to measure instant results, but the programme came to an end after just a few courses, with one of the reasons given being a lack of suitable candidates. Perhaps the work of the Lord in his workshop extended even further than we imagined!

The Eastern Daily Press cartoonist Tony Hall lets his imagination loose on the 'Joy Riders of Letton Hall'. Used with kind permission.

CHAPTER TWELVE

CONNECTING UP THE WORKSHOP

THE WATER SYSTEM

I sometimes wondered whether I should have paid more attention to my solicitor when we first purchased Letton. He pointed out that the drains from the hall appeared to lead suspiciously close to what was marked on the plans as the source of water for the house.

We assumed that since the property had been occupied for the last two hundred years by a substantial household, the services were at least adequate. We under-estimated what a major undertaking it must have been in the first place to establish a manor house, with all its trappings, right in the heart of rural Norfolk and somehow provide it with all the necessities of life. We assumed, as relative town dwellers, that water came from taps and the waste went down the drains, and we under-estimated how quickly civilised life would degenerate into something rather unsavoury when the water supply stopped altogether. Two days without water, apart from what could be begged from friends a mile or two away, left us in no fit state to operate as apprentices in the Lord's workshop, and certainly prevented us from inviting visitors to come and stay with us and share the Lord's ministry.

As we explored ways to ensure that our needs would be met, it was interesting to trace the steps our predecessors had taken over the two hundred years before we arrived, in order to provide water for the house. First of all, there were several wells around the property, as well as tanks and sumps to collect rain water. There were also large underground tanks in the stables to collect the water that ran off after the horses had been washed down.

One of the best preserved wells was a beautifully constructed brick shaft, about two metres in diameter and perhaps ten metres deep, in the corner of what John Soane had built as the laundry and brewhouse, on the ground floor of our Courtyard Flat. But the water at the bottom seemed contaminated with debris and mud, and we rejected it as an appropriate source of supply for our own use. Perhaps we were rather hasty in dismissing it as merely a historic curiosity, as there was a very old pump mounted over the well powered by an ancient electric motor, which should have given us the clue that it had been in use (presumably because it had been needed) in relatively recent times – but reject it we did.

Instead, on purchasing the property, we turned our attention to what the estate agents' particulars described as a "Private Water Supply." On the earliest maps, there was a spring marked in some woods about half a mile to the south of the main house. This spring fed the Blackwater river (really just a tiny stream at this point), which in turn fed into the Yare, ending up at the sea at Great Yarmouth, and this spring had obviously been used as the main source of water for Letton for many years.

A Spring House had been built over it, probably in Victorian times, producing a fascinating enclosed pool of water ten or fifteen metres across and two metres deep at the centre, where the spring itself could be seen bubbling up through the sandy bottom.

Alongside the Spring House there was evidence of how this water had been pumped up to the hall over the years, first of all by a three-cylinder pump operated by a water wheel and then after that, by a pair of Blake hydraulic rams. However, by the time we arrived, these had been discarded in favour of a reciprocating pump, operated by a single cylinder Lister diesel engine. For several years, this was our private water supply, and we developed a love-hate relationship with the Lister and its pump, going down into the woods early in the morning to wind up the flywheel and hope the engine would fire up, trusting that the pump, primed with both prayer and a bucket of water, would then do its stuff. It was all definitely apprentice work in the most traditional interpretation of the term.

We were keenly aware all the time that a regular and reliable supply of water was absolutely vital to the work of the Lord at Letton, so when we began to fear that the Spring House, and the spring itself, were showing signs of deterioration, we decided to undertake a major Spring House Project. This was only possible thanks to some generous gifts from supporters, and involved building a road through the woods and over some really soft and boggy ground, before we could even start work on the Spring House itself.

The walls of the Spring House were collapsing.

*The start of the Spring House project. Getting the
materials in, down the new road.*

*The roof structure looks sound. Trustee and civil engineer
Graham Arram checks out the project.*

It was a really challenging project, involving the professional skills of many people, but at the same time it provided a great experience of working together at a really practical level in the Lord's service. And who would have thought that so much mud and wet concrete could be so much fun! More details of the project, including those who funded it and those who worked on it, are included in Appendix 19 (p.186).

Placing the shuttering, with Tim Nicholson
supervising from "on board."

Then, some clever and curious engineers who had been involved at Letton for several years thought we could go one step further in improving the water supply, and reinstate the hydraulic rams. These ingenious devices use the energy of a nearby stream to pump (or 'ram') a small quantity of water up to quite a height, or for quite a distance - in Letton's case, up fifty metres at a distance of eight hundred metres away - and do this at virtually no running cost at all. A real attraction. Some details of the project are included in Appendix 20 (p.189).

Once in operation, the rams became yet another familiar aspect of Letton's water supply for several years. One of the most evocative of the apprentice jobs, often undertaken after dark at the end of the day, was to venture into the woods to turn off the rams when they were no longer needed, when the thump of the rams pulsed through the darkness like a ghostly heartbeat.

Once water had been pumped up by whatever means from the spring, a whole new area of work opened up as the water then needed to be distributed throughout the property. Initially, this included supplying areas of the farm as well as the hall, but it was quickly agreed that we had enough problems with people, without taking on responsibility for animals too, and neither did the farm want to rely on our efforts so the system was separated.

The first stage of distribution was to pump the water up to the water tower, where it had sufficient height to flow throughout the house. This water tower had been very substantially built from reinforced concrete around 1920 and although showing signs of aging when we arrived, still had plenty of life left, serving us without much trouble (until it froze), as well as pleasing the Fire Service by providing approximately twenty thousand gallons of water on hand, in case of need.

Almost finished.

The next problem was not with the tower itself, but what happened to the water while it was getting there. The Local Authority had inspected the system shortly after we moved in and had given their approval for the quality of the water "at present," but had advised us that we needed to have the water checked regularly. All went well initially, but after a few marginal water quality results we decided to carry out regular chlorine treatment, first of all by introducing chlorine into the flow from the spring, using an appropriately sized milk-bottle, and then later on by a small chlorination plant.

Again, all went well, but it was against a background of increasing standards imposed generally by Environmental Health Authorities, with whom we kept up a regular dialogue. It was interesting that throughout all this, the health of the acclimatised Letton residents was good, as had been the case (presumably) over the previous two hundred years. But, as awareness was heightened, so our need for action increased. We installed an ultra-violet light system over which incoming water flowed, killing bacteria as it did so, but then came the question: "What happens if bugs are hiding behind a particle of dirt, so don't get killed by the UV?" Then, the next question: "What happens if the electrical power fails?" Cut-outs had to be installed.

This meant that when a power cut happened, or if there was any kind of electrical problem in, for instance, the kitchen, the water would shut off and would need to be reset before normal life could be restored. Our electricity cut-outs were set at a sensitive level for extra security, so it was not uncommon to be in the dark and without water, all at once. At times, the image of 18th century life, dipping a bucket into the well, seemed very attractive.

But what might have been acceptable for residents, who had built up a resistance to local conditions, wouldn't be acceptable for visitors arriving from relatively purer places. One group of visitors remain in mind, who drank from an outside tap in the grounds, which had somehow bypassed all the UV protection. So many members of the group suffered from a tummy bug that the local GP Dr Dickie, perhaps looking for some extra interest in his quiet Norfolk practice, deemed it an epidemic. He felt obliged to make regular 'ward rounds' of the languishing teenagers, who were holding hands from bed to bed. And, once designated as an epidemic, it needed to be recorded and investigated - a process that went on for weeks after what had, after all, been only a three-day problem!

Whenever questions arose over the water supply, we considered once again some of the wider options. Could we link into Anglian Water's mains, for instance, and let them do the worrying? But since there was no mains pipeline nearby, that was prohibitively expensive. Another option was to sink a borehole and obtain our water supply in this way but although many of our neighbours did this, there were several possible disadvantages. The treatment that would be required was an unknown factor, and maybe our spring water was of better quality anyway. Also, we would be dependant more than ever on an external source of electricity.

However, the Local Authority became increasingly concerned that some further action should be taken, so much so that they eventually offered us up to £3000 if we changed our supply to a borehole. We took this as a clear signal that they would not leave us alone until we started drilling !

So, despite nearly twenty years of improving test results from our spring water system, we sank a borehole – and the first taste of that water was absolutely horrible! It improved with treatment of course, and at first the borehole water was pumped up to the water tower via its treatment plant. The authorities, however, were still concerned that contamination might creep into the system via the tower, so that too was eliminated from the supply chain. It would be good to think that all requirements have now been met but, as in so many areas of operation, general standards are continually being tightened, so we have to resign ourselves to an ongoing chase after a moving target. Perhaps it's good that as apprentices we merely have to carry out the task set before us and leave other imponderable matters to the Master.

THE DRAINS

What applies to water being supplied to Letton also applies, to a certain extent, to water being taken away. Once again, there was a bland assurance in the estate agents' Particulars of Sale that there was a "Drainage disposal system" and once again, we felt we could assume that this aspect had been dealt with satisfactorily over the two hundred years prior to our arrival. But one of the first questions to answer was, "Where?"

We could see a pattern of rectangular stone and concrete covers in a line across the side park, to the east of the house, that looked as if it might be relevant, but nothing after that. The covers were extremely heavy to move and at first sight, didn't reveal very much, except a wet and rather smelly sludge underneath them. However, as we became better and intimately acquainted – reluctantly and only when there was no other option – we discovered that we had a series of very large tanks, which corresponded to early designs for settlement and digestion systems. In theory, solids would settle in these tanks and allow a clear liquid to flow out at the far end. But again, the question was, "Where to?" Following the line of the pipe coming out of the last tank led us into the woods, where our spring was, and once again I remembered the cautionary words of my solicitor before we signed to buy.

We reasoned that there must be an outlet somewhere, and eventually we discovered some overgrown filter beds. Sure enough, there was an outlet pipe running into the little Blackwater river, thankfully several metres downstream from our spring. But it was a close thing! We also discovered a drain, beautifully built out of brick, looking as if it might have been constructed around two hundred years before, running from the house to the river, this time well upstream from our water source. We hoped that this was now merely for harmless rainwater, no matter what its original purpose might have been.

Having located the route of our drainage system, we had to accept the fact that our surplus water had to run down half a mile of rather ancient pipe work before it ran into the river. After that, it became no longer our responsibility and was hopefully treated to an acceptable standard. We were able to forget about this for most of the time, but one day, after a particularly wet spell, we heard that the ground around the Lodge (more or less on the line of the outfall pipe) was very soggy and rather wetter than might have been expected.

We explored some more heavy drain covers and came to the conclusion that our outlet pipe must be blocked across the road from our property, and about a quarter of a mile into a ploughed field. This was far beyond the reach of our own drain rods, skilled though we had become in using them, and we called in professionals.

"No problem," was the initial response but, after their largest four-wheel drive vehicle got stuck in the middle of a very muddy field for several days, their assessment changed. After waiting a while, until things had dried out a little, a second vehicle was despatched onto the field and happily succeeded both in rescuing the first one and also unblocking the drain. Roots had penetrated a cracked pipe and produced a dense plug of vegetation about two metres long. Once that was removed and the pipe repaired, our waste started to flow to the right place again ... but only for the time being, we realised.

Most of our drainage problems were much closer to home. For instance, before the stable buildings could be used residentially and re-christened as the much better-sounding Dolphin Court, we had to install proper drains. We looked in vain for any signs of previous drainage systems but found nothing, and it remained a mystery what arrangements had existed for grooms, stable lads and chauffeurs, and for the army during World War II. We resigned ourselves to installing a completely new system.

Once again, it was a steep learning curve, and not what we initially imagined we had signed up for as apprentices in the Lord's spiritual workshop. Nevertheless, eventually we managed to get the onion-shaped sewage treatment tank buried in the hole we had excavated for it, when all it wanted to do was float on the water in the bottom of the hole and bob up to well above ground level.

Levels were an ongoing problem we had to deal with, because the effluent from the Dolphin Court 'onion' had to flow into the drains outside the main hall, and there was not much height difference to help the fluid to flow. One method we devised was to couple up a fire engine pump to Fergy the tractor's power-take-off and, with the aid of fire hoses we had scrounged from our local fire service, pump the effluent to a point where it would naturally flow away.

This worked, but it wasn't at all a nice job to perform as, quite apart from the smell, everything had to be washed out afterwards, including the fire hoses that the firemen would expect to be clean if they ever had to use them for a fire. Eventually, we installed submerged electric pumps that were (amazingly) prepared to work under filthy water for years on end without attention, which surely was an example to us of selfless humble service! They came at a cost of course, but after a generous local family donated the first one to us, we made sure we put money aside for others as they became necessary.

Sometimes, the problem of levels worked the other way round, and we had far too much difference in height to contend with. One particular toilet on the first floor of the main hall discharged straight into the drains via a 150mm diameter lead pipe (known as 'six inches' when it was installed!) that went out through the wall and wound down over the roof until it went into a manhole at ground level.

Naturally, as most toilets do at some point in their lives, one day this toilet blocked. We could not release the blockage from inside the toilet bowl, or from its double-bend, no matter how hard we tried. There was no access point at all in the lead pipe as it descended over the roof and gradually we came to realise that we would have to cut into the pipe to create an access point near to the ground. Thoughts of what might be contained in ten metres of 150mm lead pipe had to be banished from our minds and a pilot hole drilled into the pipe.

Even a small hole can release quite a squirt of fluid if it's under pressure, but we had to persevere with a hacksaw – and with increasingly (and very unpleasantly) wet clothes – until we had made a hole big enough to clear the blockage. There is now a removable rodding out hole at the bottom of that particular down pipe! We can laugh at it now, but at the time it was a while before our faith was restored in our Lord's goodwill towards us.

ELECTRICITY AND FUEL

Apart from water coming in and going out, electricity needed to be connected up in order for the Lord's workshop to function properly. For most of its life, Letton had been heated by coal and lit by candles, but there was evidence that residents had been looking for better ways of doing things for some time. A 'Petrol-air gas system' for lighting was mentioned when the house was sold in 1915 and an engine-driven electrical generator was installed by 1920, but by the time we moved in the property was fully connected to the mains, albeit by rather small-capacity looking cables.

The mains fed into an impressive glass-fronted fuse cupboard, dating back to 1920, with big handles operating large switches. The porcelain fuse holders, with evocative labels like Boudoir and Female Servants Wing, proved a fascination. Young boys who were visiting seemed particularly interested in it and when they discovered that the sliding doors to the cupboard were openable, they could not resist seeing what happened when they pulled one of the big switches. Sadly, even the loud flash and bang and sudden darkness did not always prevent it being done a second time, even if only as a dare. So, the fuses and switch cupboard were isolated as a matter of urgency and modern distribution boxes installed throughout.

The same twelve- or fourteen-year-old boys became the yardstick by which we measured all our risk assessments and were the reason the luggage lift up the backstairs was dismantled. The lift itself was an open-sided wooden box, which could be hauled up from the cellar to the top floor by a rope going over a pulley at the top of the stairs. It had doubtless been a boon for generations of housemaids hauling up buckets of coal each morning.

The pulley made a distinctive noise when being operated and it sealed its fate one day when, hearing it running, we discovered two boys enjoying themselves, one in the cellar and the other riding up and down in the swaying open box. We were absolutely terrified, but the boy in the box casually stepped out of it twenty metres or so above the ground onto the staircase handrail, merely shrugging his shoulders when ordered to stop. The lift was dismantled shortly afterwards.

Before we installed bulk gas tanks, we had our own experience of lugging heavy fuel supplies around when our gas came in portable cylinders. They always seemed to run out at inconvenient times, and often half way through cooking a meal for fifty hungry guests, so there was an urgency about it, too.

Making up a trolley to carry the cylinders around helped, as did more sophisticated connections, but we empathised very much with the household staff around the house of a few generations before. The luggage lift they used for coal is now used to store firewood, so in one sense their work continues – but we are very much aware that there are far fewer apprentices around now than there were housemaids and servant lads then! In many ways, the old order seems to have been turned on its head and the few now serve the many, rather than the other way around. Just one of the many ways, perhaps, that the Gospel turns accepted standards upside down.

CHAPTER THIRTEEN

FINANCING THE WORKSHOP

The tone of Letton's finances had been set at Business Meeting no.1, held in December 1980, nearly a year after we had moved in. As mentioned in an earlier chapter, several concerned supporters had assumed I had considerable reserve money in my bank account – something like a million pounds, they hoped. Sadly, that was not the case!

For the first year or two, Letton's finances were bound up inextricably with the Carroll family finances. It's interesting to speculate on how we all survived, because even closer to that time I couldn't see where all the money that had been spent had come from. Insurance on Mary's life had provided a substantial sum, and a consulting contract from my old company had helped enormously, but there was still a gap which was difficult to explain easily. Somehow, God seemed to be at work in miraculous ways, supplying resources we didn't even know about.

The Letton Hall Trust – set up just four months after we moved in - was beginning to attract donations. In particular, the West Runton Dolphin Camps organisation set up an appeal, with the aim of helping the trust prepare accommodation and construct the kart track as soon as possible. The target for this appeal was an ambitious £25,000 (amounting to perhaps ten times that amount today), but the target was reached and exceeded in an impressively short time. We were enormously grateful for their help and delighted that work could start on Dolphin Court and the track straightaway. Naming Dolphin Court in recognition seemed only a small token of our gratitude.

Soon after Mary's death it was agreed to set up an additional appeal fund in her memory, with the primary aim of providing something tangible at Letton to remember her by. My faith was feeble at first, and I imagined some modest plaque somewhere, but as donations mounted we realised that a much bigger project could be envisaged. It was decided to use the money to refurbish and furnish what most visitors regarded as the best large room in the house and dedicate it as The Mary Carroll Library. It was rewired so that it could be properly lit, and redecorated, and an attractive carpet chosen and fitted – but it still lacked proper chairs by the time the money ran out.

It was at this point that we experienced yet another of the incidents that kept on cropping up, and which assured us that the Lord was looking after us with great love and care. The treasurer of the Mary Carroll Appeal Trust phoned up to say that they had under-estimated the amount of tax due back from covenanted giving and there were now several hundred pounds available. "Could we think of an appropriate way in which this money could be used?"

At about the same time, we had been given details of a company in Huntingdon that specialised in hotel furniture and yes, they had a stock of library chairs in at the moment, but not many. We had already calculated the number of chairs we needed – and when we checked, we found that they had exactly that number, and that the money we had received just covered this purchase. But final confirmation came once the chairs arrived and we discovered that their colour just matched a key background colour in the carpet. Perfect! It wasn't only the fact that we now had chairs in the room that gave us so much satisfaction and encouragement, but even more was the knowledge that our gracious and meticulously caring God had arranged a colour match too.

Apart from these major contributions, there were also many other smaller donations, as mentioned earlier, which helped and encouraged us in the very early days. One such offering, which can perhaps speak for many others, was the one shown in the letter pictured below from two young brothers: £1.02, to go with their prayers for Letton. Never mind the amount, the value was incalculable.

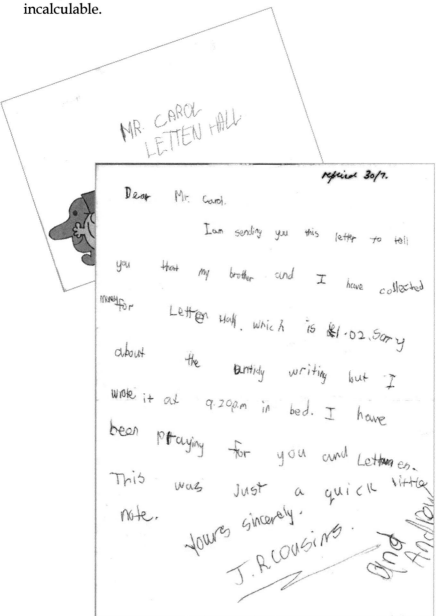

When the new trustees joined the Letton Hall Trust at the start of 1982, they brought with them further professional expertise and wholehearted Christian commitment rather than a large sum of money, as some had hoped. But this was very much in keeping with how the Lord obviously intended his workshop to be funded. It was a venture of faith rather than a mere allocation of money that was already in the bank. And one of the first requirements was careful use of resources.

In Exodus, chapter 4, God instructs Moses in how to carry out His plan.

"What is that in your hand?" said the Lord.

"A staff," replied Moses.

"Then use it," was the essence of the Lord's reply. "This is so that they may believe that the Lord has appeared to you." (Exodus 4:1-5)

This quotation appeared at the top of a sheet of paper addressed to the Letton team, listing: "What we can do *now*, even if we had no more money coming in for the next few weeks. What is in our hands?"

* *Rubbish – remove it!*
* *Paint – spread it!*
* *Guttering – hang it! [a large quantity had just been delivered]*
* *Tools – use them!*
* *Nails etc – hit them!*
* *Food in store – eat it!*
* *Each other – hold together in love!*
* *Praying friends – inform them!*

Attached to this piece of paper was a more detailed and specific list of jobs that needed to be done when resources permitted. One of these was the need to erect a stud wall next to the newly erected staircase, between the first and second floors of the main hall, to form a new bedroom, to be called Peterborough. Someone had costed up the materials needed for this job on a scrap of paper (see illustration) at £76.29, which was not much at all to create a new bedroom, but the rule was "no projects until we have the money," so the job could not be done.

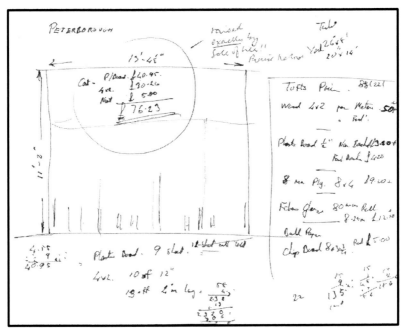

The Peterborough Bedroom "Costing Sheet."

One of the clearing up jobs included on the list was the removal of a pile of old roof tiles, left over when a rotting shed had been demolished to make room for construction of the kart track. It was agreed that I should approach a local dealer, just in case he might be interested in taking them off our hands and, to my delight, he seemed quite keen. He and a mate came over to Letton and sorted and counted them out, and with the requisite head-scratching and gloomy muttering, gave me a price. I could hardly believe my ears, because it covered the cost of creating the Peterborough bedroom exactly, to the nearest pound. It seemed churlish not to accept the cash straightaway, without even attempting to bargain! On the illustration of the costing sheet, there is a note that I added at the time: "Raised <u>exactly</u> by sale of tiles!! Praise the Lord"

JUST-IN-TIME PROVISION

There was always a tension between wanting to spend money on improvements and needing to husband and consolidate our resources. Should we spend or should we save? "We need full occupancy, but to achieve this we need to spend money on improvements."

For several years, the financial report at each trust meeting concluded that we needed £5000 just to survive, and certainly could not consider carrying out new projects, no matter how attractive they appeared. It's interesting to look back and see how it always seemed to be around the same amount: just too much to raise easily in human terms, yet not too much to hope and pray for. It's comforting to look back now with the perspective of time and know that we *did* survive, but when we were living through those situations for real, they were extremely difficult. How *did* we survive? They were times of nail-biting, of questioning whether we were right in attempting to persevere; times of sleepless nights and pretty desperate prayers.

When grants or gifts came in, it was not only the financial value that was important, but also the fact that they confirmed time and time again that we could trust the Lord, so long as we were constantly seeking his will and attempting to carry it out. Several donations came from trusts, including the Jerusalem Trust who helped us on several occasions, thanks to the support of local trustees.

One of our first donations came from the Anne French Trust, administered by the Bishop of Norwich, and we also received grants to fund the Adventure Trail in the woods from The Princes Trust and from BBC's Children in Need programme. Not to be outdone, Anglia Telethon also provided a grant to help in improving the accommodation in Dolphin Court, including a timber roof lining in the loft areas. And of course, the £25,000 from the West Runton Appeal enabled us to make a start with the whole project.

In the early 1980s, we made two formal and general appeals, setting out what we felt was a good case for help and support. We circulated them widely, but response was so limited that we concluded that it was not the Lord's will to finance his workshop in this way. It seemed that we were putting all our human skills into making a persuasive and attractive appeal, and approaching all the likely sources with well-produced brochures. But while we were doing this, God was working behind our backs, arranging for funding to come from individual Christians whose hearts he had touched.

One example of this sticks in my mind. We had decided that the Go-Kart track needed resurfacing and widening in places but we could not afford the estimated £10,000 to do this, and time was running out before the summer season began. We had worked hard at fund-raising, but there was still a gap we could not bridge. We had held a Day of Prayer on a Saturday in June, but by that Sunday evening I was preparing myself for the gloomy task of calling off the project on Monday morning.

Then, the telephone rang. It was David Ham, rather than a trustee of one of the large grant-making trusts we had been approaching, and I prepared myself for a friendly chat about routine matters – which we had. But then Dave said he and his wife had been left some money by a relative and wanted to help Letton: "How much did we need to carry out the kart track project?" The gap was bridged and we started the work almost immediately! God had indeed been working behind our backs while we struggled on in our own strength.

Another instance came about from a casual conversation which I seem to recall took place outside our kitchen window. But whatever the circumstances, the outcome was a very generous donation from Chris and Maggie Paterson. In my letter of thanks to them I said, "On Tuesday I'd drawn up a plan of action that seemed to lead inevitably to having to sell Letton ... then on Wednesday you made your wonderful offer – and now by Thursday evening the way ahead is clear, at least for the next step."

They were desperate times indeed, but once again the Lord prompted his people. Although once again, we were only shown one step at a time and had to go forward in faith to the next one.

There are far too many more people to list fully here, but nearly every issue of Letton News contained names of individuals who had helped Letton over that period, either financially or in kind, or by skilled and expert time spent at Letton. Mention of individual names will only ensure that many names are missed off, but it's difficult to ignore how often the names occur of Tim Nicholson, David Morgan, Richard Simpson, Andrew Whadcoat and Charlie Woods, all of whom gave their skilled time.

All the donations and practical help from individuals came against the background of a generally tight financial situation, with the regular cry ringing out that, "We need £5,000 to be able to continue." The passage of time has taken the sting out of that urgent plea, but they were very real and testing situations. There was always, of course, the last-resort option of closing down and selling up, but each time we considered that action, we came to the prayerful conclusion that the Lord was doing a great work at Letton Hall and we needed to press on, even if we could not see a human way through.

Letton News no.19 has this comment from the trustees:

"A lot of blessing in the past at Letton has come when in financial terms we could do nothing other than trust in the Lord's provision – sometimes in the tightest of situations. So we are encouraged to go on trusting Him."

So, given those circumstances, when individuals or trusts made donations, they were agents of the Lord's provision and, in a very real sense, saving Letton. That gives them a very special place in Letton's history, and often means that Letton also has a special place in their lives.

Despite the ongoing battle to meet running costs and make necessary improvements, the underlying aim for the trust to buy Letton remained, because it made sense in every way. Yet for twenty-five years it seemed an impossible aim and we had to struggle on, setting up various leases that gave a measure of security and, at the same time, took into account what the trust was spending on improving the property. The Carroll family were very happy to sell, but wanted to stay faithful to the original vision and for the Lord to continue in his workshop; and Letton was also their family home. The facts and the figures just didn't seem to add up.

Then, slowly, the situation changed, as the Lord's timing arrived. I retired as Director of the trust at the end of 2002 at the age of sixty-five. Two years before that, Kay and I and the family had moved to live in central Norwich, feeling that there were other "Resident Couples" in place by that time and also, that our own living accommodation was needed for more staff. We had always felt that it would be best not to continue living at Letton after retirement but to allow the new team freedom from someone saying, "That's not the way to do it." The move to Norwich was the start of that process. The provision of ideal rented accommodation there was another example to us of the

Lord's timely provision and in a sense, prepared us for other changes in store, including my "release from indentures" as an apprentice to the Lord.

Gradually, the trust was able to build up financial reserves and we negotiated a selling price so that they could launch a new campaign to purchase. The price was based on a professional valuation, coupled with what we assessed we needed to live on after we had discharged our own mortgage. The figure we came up with was £960,000, against a valuation of £1.25m, and we gave the trust a two-year option at this price to allow time to raise this sum.

Letton News no.41 (see Appendix 21, p.191) sets out the situation with about six months left before the two-year deadline expired, with still an enormous gap to bridge. An "Urgent Appeal" letter sent out with only two months to go, records good progress but still a shortfall between what was in the bank and what income was required to service a mortgage. Finally, Letton News no.43, dated April 2007 (see Appendix 22, p.192) tells the blow-by-blow story of the previous few days, before the purchase was finally made ... and, as John Currey says in his account, "The last two years were a roller-coaster ride." How typical this nail-biting last-minute pattern was of the Lord's plans working out, testing faith to the limit – yet how much greater was the rejoicing that came with victory!

The Carroll family were, of course, well away from the front-line action by this time and could only watch from the side-lines. But from our point-of-view, we could only marvel at what the Lord was achieving through his people. We remembered how he had made it so clear at the start that we should purchase this 'crumbling wreck' that was to be "A house for the Lord and a Home for His People."

How many misgivings we had had about the Lord's choice of property from the human outlook of investment value, yet how wise He had been proved. How impossible it had seemed, over the twenty-five years of our apprenticeship (for most of those years working without a salary), to think about financial provision for the future. And yet, here we were, being presented with the means to obtain a reasonable pension after paying off the mortgage. God was indeed good!

CHAPTER FOURTEEN

APPRENTICES AND THEIR INDENTURES

How valid does my picture seem, of life at Letton Hall being an apprenticeship to the Lord in his workshop?

First of all, it is a picture that I would only apply to myself. Others who have been or remain at Letton may have very different views of their own service there. But for me, it is a picture that seems to fit the situation in many ways, incorporating a sense of learning all the time from the Master and being in a privileged position to see Him at work. That sense of privilege is even greater when the Master shares some of his work with His apprentice.

The concept of apprenticeship seems to be enjoying something of a vogue at present, but some of its older characteristics can add something to the idea too. The basic definition has always been that it is a period of training where an apprentice commits himself to a master, who in turn pledges to teach and train him. But in earlier years, it was set out in a formal legal agreement: an Indenture. The following extract is from an agreement made between one Charles Lee and a "carver and guilder," James Dracott, in 1802, and gives an idea of what was involved:

> *This Indenture witnesseth that Charles Lee ... doth put himself apprentice to James Dracott ... and with him to serve. During the term the said apprentice his said Master faithfully shall serve, his secrets keep, his lawful commands everywhere gladly do. He shall do no damage to his said Master, nor see to be done*

of others ... he shall not waste the goods of his said Master ... but in all things as a faithful apprentice he shall behave himself towards his said Master. And the said Master shall teach and instruct, or cause to be taught and instructed in the best manner he can, finding unto the said apprentice meat, drink, apparel, washing and lodging, and other necessaries according to the custom of the City of London.

There is a lot more in the agreement about, for instance, not haunting taverns and playing at dice or cards etc, but there seems quite a lot (as well as this) that is absolutely relevant to Letton Hall. I find it particularly interesting to learn how the agreement was drawn up physically and what it looked like. It was in two halves, one to be kept by the apprentice and one by the Master. The two halves were originally drawn up on a single sheet of parchment and then separated by a wavy cut (an "indented" cut) so that they could be matched together; and that way, it was certain that the agreement between apprentice and Master was one and the same document. It was personal and unique to the two of them.

At Letton Hall, the Lord has displayed great skill in matching up the people to work for him there. I can only speak from my own personal experience, but it seems that my own brand of positive optimism, pressing on – some would say blundering on! – despite disappointments and problems, seeing opportunities and enlisting help, was just right for the early pioneer phases of Letton. But that attitude needed to have others around to bring order out of a dreamer's chaos, giving attention to detail and compliance with the ever increasing flow of rules and regulations. And God supplied such people!

I felt the need particularly strongly after the death of Mary, who as an organiser and fixer, covered in many ways for my own shortcomings. We needed not only project people who responded to the excitement of new things, but also patient workers who made sure that the necessary day-to-day routines were carried out. And most of all, we needed people whose faith and spiritual discernment would keep us looking to the Lord. For me personally, Kay supplied that spiritual orientation.

As I write this, the faces and names come flooding in of people who were and are specially appointed by the Lord to fulfil His work at Letton. It is an impossible task for me to list names for such a complex "human resources" scheme, but the Lord controlled it and provided the people.

They included volunteers who visited for perhaps just a few days, and people who thought they were just coming for a short time but ended up spending months and even years at Letton. Some people came with a very clear sense of call and others came at a needy time of their lives, wondering what they could contribute, yet filling a vital role and at the same time growing in a sense of their own value. It was such a thrilling aspect of the Lord at work in his workshop.

Janet Adams and Harry - our Millennium Garden volunteer - getting their hands dirty.

Apprentices come and go; it's in the very nature of the agreement. It seems apprenticeships can be really short, but sometimes last a lifetime, in the same way that "Old accountants never die, they just lose their balance" or "Old photographers never die, they just go to the old focus home." So, perhaps "Old apprentices never die, they just lose their (in)dentures!"

The thought that an apprenticeship does not have to be a life sentence makes it easier to move on, and I suspect that most people who have moved on from Letton have done so with a sense that they have completed their time and can go with an easy heart. Again, names and situations are too many to single out, but some have gone on to fulfil a wider ministry and some to go back to what they were doing before spending a season at Letton. Some, like me, have genuinely retired, only to find other things to do on the basis that there is no retirement from the Lord's service.

What is so good to see, for all who have been or stayed at Letton, is that the Lord himself is still at work in his workshop, as can be seen in the continuing stream of issues of Letton News still being composed.

Lord Jesus Christ, Master Carpenter of Nazareth,
who through the cross of wood and nails has wrought
man's full salvation,
Wield well your tools in this your workshop
that we who come to you rough hewn may be fashioned
to a truer and fuller beauty,
in your name and for your glory.
Amen

APPENDICES

APPENDICES CONTENTS

I

TASK FORCE 81

LETTON HALL

PSALM 127 : 1 & 2   *"Unless the Lord*
boilds the house..."

Shipdham,
Thetford,
Norfolk.
Telephone: Dereham (0362) 820717

NEWS

20 JANUARY 1981

OF THE NEW YEAR AT LETTON

In early December we held a weekend get-together (with both formal and informal aspects) of people representing many of those involved in using Letton and in working here. The outcome of this — after much prayer & discussion — has been the setting up of

TASK FORCE 81

The aim is to unite, in a planned & organised way, the various talents & abilities of people with a commitment, under the Lord, to Letton; to focus them into a limited period concentrating first on a "start-of-the-season" date of 10 April; then operating and improving things through 'til the end of the summer.

After this, an ongoing management structure will be developed. The structure of the Letton Hall Trust is also being worked on to bring it up-to-date.

The tasks to be tackled have been divided up with each area under a *TASK FORCE LEADER* who is setting up his or her FORCE. The Task Force leaders share all the major aspects of running Letton, meeting regularly with Peter Carroll as chairman —
They are :

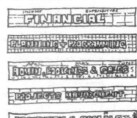

Philip Doyne — FINANCIAL

Tony Collis — PLANNING & PROGRAMMING

Sonia Knight — FOOD, SUPPLIES & SALES

Geoff. Sussex — BUILDING & EQUIPMENT

Peter Carroll. — PROMOTION & APPEALS

Task Force is well under way and progress is encouragingly good. Many people are (or will be!) involved — don't be surprised if it's you!

TRUSTEE PROFILE: SONIA KNIGHT

Team Profile ....

LN 12 p4

If you have visited Letton or made a booking to stay here, or placed a food order, or spent a day working here, you have almost certainly met Sonia Knight (or receive a letter from her, or sampled her amazing cooking .....), because in many respects Sonia is the base on which our administration and day to day running depends.

After her conversion in her home county of Suffolk, Sonia moved to Wales where she was baptised and spent three years working with a local church. In that time she was accepted as Wales first single foster mum .... brave lady ! However, a Christian witness to alcoholics which Sonia operated from her home didn't meet with approval from neighbours who managed to bring an end to that avenue of service.

Back in Suffolk, having prayed about the way ahead, she was unsure about returning to Wales to accept teenage foster children until really sure of God's will. This was confirmed when Sonia visited her uncle, Major Bill Batt, who had heard of Letton's need for an administrator/secretary. Within a week, Sonia had seen Peter Carroll at Letton and both Peter and Sonia knew the Lord's clear leading — and within another month she had sold up in Wales and was resident at Letton !

This was all back in the autumn of 1980. After eighteen months of living at Letton, Sonia was able to put down roots in a lovely house in Shipdham, and as a result, our links with the community have greatly benefitted.

We often say, perhaps lightly, that the Lord never forsakes or leaves us. Sonia's testimony is that she has experienced the wonderful truth of His great faithfulness and active love.

RESIDENT COUPLE PROFILE: ALAN AND ENID ROBERTS

Enid was one of the very first visitors to Letton, coming in early 1980 (with June Rootham), as reported in Letton News:

> ... to find out what the mysterious new owner Peter Carroll was up to. They found out that he was a Christian seeking to establish Letton as a Christian Centre. They also found that he was keen to involve local Christians in the project and that he was very good at finding things for people to do - and the rest is history!

At her retirement in 2007 Letton News said:

> The work has been blessed by her gentle gracious style of service ever since. As well as the accounts, bookings and a myriad of administrative tasks, Enid has always been willing to help with whatever needs to be done.

Tragically, Enid died in a road accident a few years later, but it is recorded that after her 'retirement' she:

... returned as a volunteer ... and laid out two knot gardens in the Italian Garden ... with box hedges, lavender and standard roses. Gifts received in her memory have paid for two very substantial and impressive teak benches to be installed in the area she devoted so much time to. In the early days of Letton, Enid and Alan spent over two years as resident wardens, living almost entirely by faith, because the Trust was unable to support them properly.

Alan and Enid.

The Letton News at that time said that *"practically every weekend was booked so there wasn't much time for anything other than routine work."* Nevertheless, Alan was described as the man with "miracles at his fingertips" and adds:

Another major step forward has been the installation of heating in the bedroom wing of Dolphin Court. Alan achieved this at incredibly low cost using a boiler and radiators he found tucked away unused in a forgotten corner. The new system has transformed the life of those using Dolphin Court and has greatly extended the season during which the Court can be booked.

This job was typical of the work Alan undertook in the early pioneering days of Letton when funds were very limited. It involved mastering all aspects of water supply, plumbing, drainage and sewage treatment, and extended to building and decorating projects all over the property - anything, in fact, that was either technical or mechanical. There are many examples of Alan's work around Letton but one abiding impression remains - his quiet Christian witness, backed up by well-thumbed bible in the corner of his workshop, to all who worked with him.

TRUSTEE PROFILE: GRAHAM ARRAM

Trustee Graham Arram is the name on 10,000 letterheads, in his capacity as secretary to Letton Hall Trust ... and he finds himself in this role because a few months ago he prayed to the Lord for an outlet for some energies he felt still might be available even after his involvement with the church in Thundersley and his career !

Career, for Graham at present, is as an engineer with Castle Point District Council, responsible for civil engineering contracts up to £1 million and beyond, with special emphasis on projects dealing with water. Before this, Graham was in partnership in a private civil engineering consultancy, after other local authority work, following training at Kingsway College and the Mid-Essex Technical College.

Graham's links with Letton started only after 17 yrs latterly as secretary, with the organization now known as S.E.Essex Christian Houseparties. When Ollie Thatcher first met Graham (through a close link between Ollie's wife and Graham's mum) he set a chain of fast reactions going, ending in a meeting at Letton in November '81 when an amazing total of sixteen busy people from various groups and contacts, found they were free to come. After much prayer and prayerful discussion at this gathering and at later meetings, a group of men and women came together as the new trustees of Letton Hall Trust — with Graham as the secretary.

Graham's wife Ann, with children Paul, Mark, Dawn and Andrew (born October 24th '81) have stayed at Letton on a number of occasions (brave family !) and are supporting him in his involvement here. Let us also support him and his family by our prayers for all that they will need in this task he is undertaking for the Lord.

5

TRUSTEE PROFILE: THE CARROLL FAMILY

Kay was one of the first Lettoneers arriving the summer of 1980 just in time to help with the final stages of building the Kart Track. Despite feeling the strong leading of the Lord to Letton, she had no idea then of her long time future here!

Peter has the doubtful privilege of being the longest serving resident of present day Letton having moved in on 1 December 1979. The seven years since then have been eventful, action-packed, often nail-biting, but always with the Lord's hand upon them.

Life since leaving his previous role as Managing Director and Chairman of Panavista Ltd has been marked by a series of steps of faith, the latest one being on 1 July this year when the family became dependent on Letton for their livihood. Mission England is now completely finished, Peter's contract with Panavista completed its term at the end of June - and full commitment to Letton seemed the right course of action. But it is a step of faith .....

The ownership of Letton and the legal solution now seems settled. There are no immediate signs of the Trust being able to buy the property so ownership remains with the Carrolls - but the Trust has a lease and additional protection for the money it spends on improvements, (an "extra" not always included in leases). Peter is negotiating a mortgage as a stable and economic way of replacing the bank loan raised to cover initial developments. The rent being received under the lease just about covers the mortgage payments - so some of the uncertainty surrounding these aspects over recent years seems about to be resolved.

Jonathan is now into his second year teaching at Gosfield School near Halstead and is a relatively rare visitor to Letton. Simon is settling into Medical School life at Newcastle (although playing an increasingly prominent part in Kart Camp life here). Bridget hopes to return before Christmas with what we are sure will be amazing tales of 12 months in Australia. (LATEST NEWS — she's back now!)

Gran continues to lead a busy social life in the neighbourhood despite feeling the rigours of winter weather rather more these days, and continues to dispense her excellent hospitality whenever she can.

The younger members of the family, Jenny and Rachel, venture out more and more to the "groups" who play such a prominent part in their lives. For those with an eye for future developments, there is another Carroll due in 1987 - although Kay maintains (stoutly!) that only the very sharp eyed could detect it at present.

TRUSTEE PROFILE:
JOHN AND MARGARET CURREY

TRUSTEE PROFILE Nº 4

Most people just visit Letton for a week or two then go
back to their own homes - but trustees John and Margaret
Currey with Matthew and Janice came to Letton nearly 4
years ago and moved jobs and home to be near here.

John is the Letton Hall Trust Treasurer and it has been his persistent, wise, and cool-
headed work on the finances that has piloted Letton through what seems to be frequently
difficult waters. The lights often burn late in the office when John is working on
the accounts and the correspondence and calculations that go with them, and we owe him
a great debt of gratitude. John is now Managing Director of a Dereham firm building
advanced-design truck bodies for customers all over the UK and we ask you to pray for
his work and witness in this demanding role as well as for his Letton Treasurership.

Margaret's contribution to Letton is enormously valuable too, and she is regularly seen
leading in groups of ladies armed with brushes and mops and polishing cloths to do
battle with the dust and dirt. Letton is a big house both to clean and to make into a
home, and countless homemaking touches we owe to Margaret, from bedspreads to pictures
on the wall. We also thank Margaret for being an encourager and a willing taker-on-of-
tasks when everyone else is flagging!

Margaret and John and family now worship at Dereham Baptist Church where John is a
Deacon. Before moving here they worshipped at Fairlop Evangelical Church in Ilford
and at that time John worked with the Times Newspaper Group.

They have encouraged many folk from both their present and past churches to visit
Letton, and have been leading lights in organising events such as the Summer Break.

TRUSTEE PROFILE: GWYN JORDAN

LETTON NEWS Nº 23 AUTUMN 1993

TRUSTEE PROFILE Nº 7 Gwyn Jordan

"Not so much a country house" thought Gwyn Jordan when he first saw Letton "more an ancient monument". Nevertheless, in Nov 1981, in company with (bro.) Garfield Jordan, Graham Arram and Phil Webb, he consented to become a Trustee. Perhaps it was the trees that took his fancy, or the chance to indulge his gardening and natural history hobbies ....? Whatever, we were very pleased to have his contribution in what he clearly identified as a "venture of faith".

Gwyn is a professional scientist, a lecturer at King's College London, researching in the area of cell biology; and - this year - has spent 6 months working in the Norwich Science Park, using the electron and other microscope facilities of the John Innes Centre.

Letton has benefited from this period too. Gwyn's contribution as a Trustee is unique and very valuable - and the more we have of it, the better! He too is a "rotating chairman" with gifts of discernment and sensitivity that have often helped us to get to the heart of issues. He also has the ability to produce creative and spiritual solutions when everyone else fears we're at a dead end!

Dr. Gwyn Jordan.

Gwyn spends a lot of his time preaching and teaching, often visiting different churches (as well as organising camps and houseparties with sailing, canoeing, fell-walking etc in different parts of the country) so it's quite surprising to find he's still where he started. He and Doreen are in fellowship at Thundersley Gospel Hall where he remembers (he claims!) being in the Sunday School aged around 7! Now it is the open form of worship in the Breaking of Bread that he treasures particularly.

Daughters Rachel and Jane seem to be following the same pattern, maintaining home roots whilst travelling far and wide, with Rachel just returned to the UK after 2 years with YWAM in Amsterdam, and a year with Streetlife for Norwich YFC, and Jane currently doing a Discipleship Training Scheme with YWAM after teaching in local schools.

Gwyn is the last of the original trustees to be "profiled" but then Jesus had something to say about who comes first and last didn't he?

TRUSTEE PROFILE: MARTIN LODGE

LETTON NEWS   Nº 23   AUTUMN 1993

– 6 –

TRUSTEE PROFILE Nº 6   Martin Lodge

Martin has been a Trustee of Letton since the Trust was set up in its present form in Jan 1982 – having first visited on a bleak November day in 1981, at the instigation of Phil Webb.

At that time Martin was working at Plessey as an engineer having graduated in Electronics Engineering at London University a dozen or so years earlier. Thus he was able to add yet more skills to the already wide range offered by the other trustees.

Over the succeeding years, though, it hasn't only been his practical abilities we've appreciated, but just as much his wisdom and God-guided common sense in all sorts of areas. As "rotating-chairman" at Trust meetings (just what do Trustees get up to ..?!) he will insist that we take time to listen to the Lord in prayer, – and yet still try to finish before midnight! His involvement has been very much a family affair, including for instance with Marcia, Andrew(14), Amy(11), and Anna(8) hosting a Christmas Houseparty here.

Martin with Andrew, Amy and Anna.

Although Martin is born and bred a Yorkshireman, he has lived in Dagenham for 20 years, and since 1984, has been in business with Geoff Webb as Wedge Motors. This involves sales and general motor engineering – and as well as sponsoring some of Letton's karting, it has also included supplying several cars to Norfolk (so .... if you're "in the market" try 081 595 6618 – don't forget to mention Letton Hall!!)

When Martin first moved to Dagenham, he joined Lillechurch – now Dagenham Community Church where he still worships as part of the Leadership team. It's this church that he will be bringing to Letton over New Year 1993/4, and by all accounts, filling both the Hall and Dolphin Court to absolute bursting point.

Thank you, Martin and family, for all you are contributing to the Lord's work at Letton Hall.

TRUSTEE PROFILE: PHIL AND PAT WEBB

Twelve months ago, Phil and Pat Webb, Jenny, Peter, Emily and Honey hadn't even heard of Letton ... now they are installed (more or less !) in the Gallery Flat, and Letton Hall has become home for all of them for the foreseeable future.

This major change for them and for Letton came about only through the remarkable intervention of the Lord in their lives, but they are no strangers to this, as anyone who has heard Phil's accounts of his journeyings through Africa and the Sahara will know. It was through his "African Safari" that Phil got to know Pat, whose parents were missionaries in Central Africa.

With family responsibilities ahead, Phil settled in to a career of teaching, having studied Zoology (just right for Letton ?) for a London Univ. B.Sc., followed by a Grad. Cert. Ed. also in London. He then taught at schools in Barking and Havering for four years. Pat continued her nursing career (having trained at Westminster, and taken midwifery qualifications at Poole) working as a midwife in Rush Green, and then training and working as a Health Visitor ... until the arrival of Jenny.

In 1976, they felt the call to work for the Lord on a full-time basis, and Phil was invited to work with the Evangelical Free Church, Lillechurch Rd, Dagenham, in evangelism and pastoral duties. This ministry was growing and keeping him very busy, when as a result of a "chance" circumstance, Phil found himself thirty miles from here with a few hours to spare. He decided to look up an old friend Don Gee ... Don was working at Letton at the time, so suggested a meeting "on site" ... and from then on the Lord began to make it progressively clearer that this was where He wanted them to be ...

TRUSTEE PROFILE:
NEIL AND JANE STARLING

LETTON NEWS

No. 33
Autumn 1999

Since last year **the Trustees** have been considering the need to have more local Trustees - *"more"* because the Trust is at least two members down on it's normal strength, and *"local"* because it's easier for local people to keep in touch and be available to support the team. At about the same time, **Neil & Jane Starling** felt that God was calling them to be involved in the work of Letton in whatever capacity was needed.

These two situations, coming about as they did, seemed to have something of the mark of a "God-incidence" about them - and certainly demanded looking into. The Trustees and Neil and Jane would very much value your prayers as events move towards final decisions.

The process hasn't been entirely straightforward up to now. Neil and Jane at present live in Rugeley which isn't "local" by any stretch of the imagination! When they put their home up for sale early in 1999, to test things out, houses everywhere else in the UK seemed to be selling on sight -but theirs didn't! However, a few weeks ago it sold, and at the same time they saw a house at nearby Hingham that fitted their needs.

Most people have to find a job in a new location before they move, but *this* part of the jigsaw seemed to fit into place straightaway. Some 18 months ago, after 12 years in teaching, Neil found he was able to work full time in his school music book publishing business, Champion House Press. Happily this business can operate from almost anywhere..! Jane's music tuition work is also "moveable"- although she is finding increasingly that she's needed to help out in the business. There's the family to look after too, with Philip aged 9 and Robert 3. In fact it is through "family" that many people will know the Starlings , as they have been regular worship leaders at Letton's Family Weeks for 9 years.

Soon after they were married Neil and Jane began leading worship together, and writing worship songs. They have recorded several albums and have led music seminars, celebrations and services in many churches since then. We hope to benefit too from some of their other talents which include degrees in music (MA), Librarianship and Religious Studies, plus a spell managing a W H Smith book department, and a keen interest in interior design ....!

Please pray for the Lord's plan to unfold clearly over the next few weeks.

RESIDENT COUPLE PROFILE:
KEN AND PAT WEBB

The Norfolk Wing
Letton Hall
Shipdham
Thetford
Norfolk   IP 25 7SA

Greetings

On July 16th we arrived at Letton Hall to start the new life that we believe God has led us to. We being Ken and Pat Webb late of Chelmsford in Essex.

Pat had left her job as a secondary school teacher at the summer half-term break after twentysix years, the last sixteen of them teaching RE.

Ken had taken voluntary redundancy after being in the computer service industry for twenty-one years (God moves in wonderful ways).

One house sale and our daughters wedding followed, then we were "ready" for Letton Hall, straight into - Family weeks - Kart camps - Saturday changeovers - Summer season - and an old "friend"...dry-rot.

Eight months later having "settled in" we are in some kind of routine, working three weekdays for Letton and "crafting" on the other two to support ourselves. Pat practises the art of pyrography, and her wedding plates are proving very sought after. Ken has transformed the old lettoneers kitchen into a workshop and a woodturning lathe now purrs away where the kitchen units used to be. Our wares are sold using the Party-plan idea, Burn-and-Turn parties now becoming part of lifes rich pattern.

Pat's influence is being felt in the house - mill owners being coerced into giving bargains of fabrics - the bedrooms now getting the colour co-ordinated treatment. Future plans include setting up national curriculum related courses for Primary/Junior school children together with G.C.S.E. field courses in various subjects.

Dolphin court's hayloft has been the recipient of some of Ken's attention, and our guests, that use the former stable block, now benefit from a central heating system.

We would like to say a big thank you to all friends who are supporters of the work at Letton. Our prayer is that you are blessed as much as our groups are.

Our present support together with group fees enables us to meet our basic running costs, but not to carry out the improvements that modern day living demands.If you would like to join our support team and become a "Friend of Letton" please return the slip from the bottom of the enclosed leaflet.

Please continue to pray for us - we really need it.

Yours in HIS service

Ken & Pat Webb

RESIDENT COUPLE PROFILE: STEPHEN AND PIPPA MAWDITT

The post of Resident Couple was advertised in the Christian press in Autumn 1987 and Stephen and Pippa Mawditt arrived in response to it to take up residency in a newly refurbished Norfolk Wing. Their enthusiasm and commitment in taking up the various roles was a great relief to the overstretched existing team. Pippa immersed herself in the housekeeping straightaway in co-ordination with the existing staff and volunteers.

Stephen set about bringing the administration into the computer age, and provided regular and comprehensive briefing reports to the trustees, encouraging them to clarify their vision for the future. A local management executive was set up and ministry to the local area explored.

The Mawditt family entertaining some of the Roothams, on the lawn at Letton.

At the same time, the Mawditts welcomed all Letton's visitors with humour and love - and many people expressed their great appreciation of their work. This extract from Letton News no.19 of Autumn 1990 tells of the sadness at their departure - yet recognising the Lord's guidance in it:

Dear Friends,

This is something of a MILESTONE EDITION of the newsletter. It marks considerable progress along the road, but reminds us that there is still a long way to go ....

One of the major milestones in recent years was the arrival of Stephen & Pippa Mawditt nearly 3 years ago, but sadly they will be leaving at the end of this year. Due partly to financial constraints, as explained later in this letter, and due partly to Stephen & Pippa's own widening vision, after a great deal of prayer and deliberation we all agreed that this is the course of action the Lord is leading us into.

When we look back on all that Stephen & Pippa have achieved, and think with excitement of all that the Lord has in store for them in the future, we can't be too gloomy about it — but it is with a real sense of sadness that we wish them well as they go.

Sharing in the Lord's service

The Trustees.

13

RESIDENT COUPLE PROFILE: GERALD AND JUNE ROOTHAM

We welcomed June and Gerald Rootham and their family formally in Letton News no.26 in March 1995, but it was very much a "welcome back." June was one of our very first visitors in 1980 when, as a neighbour living in Shipdham, she and Enid Roberts came to see what mysterious things were happening at "the big house down the road." They became helpful and committed local supporters for several years until they moved with Gerald's Building Society work to Portsmouth.

LETTON NEWS MARCH 1995

We are delighted to welcome **Gerald & June Rootham** as Warden and Housekeeper, appointed to the posts in January – after rigorous interviewing against tough competition! It's very much a "welcome back", as Gerald & June & their family – Jonathan, Simon, Sarah and Matthew – have been associated with Letton from its very beginnings. They moved away to the Portsmouth area nearly 10 years ago but felt the Lord's calling on their lives for full-time Christian service – and also eventually the call to return to Norfolk.

Since their arrival, many visitors to Letton have enjoyed June's cooking and catering skills and many areas have benefited from Gerald's painting, decorating, team-leadership and administrative skills, – and we've had the added bonus of Simon and Sarah on the team, helping with everything from shop to scalextric, and from karting to biking. We hope also to have the benefits of Jonathan's help too, during his university vacations, – plus of course Matthew's cheerful presence <u>all</u> the time!

Their roles at Letton were far reaching but their fifteen years in residence were marked, in practical terms, by a determined perseverance towards financial stability and higher housekeeping, safety and operating standards. In spiritual terms, their aims for Letton were set out in Letton News no.37:

In the midst of their busy and demanding lives, Gerald felt the call to train for ordained ministry in the Church of England, and somehow found time to carry this through, as recorded in Letton News no.33:

Rootham family news...

Starting at the younger end, **Matthew** is enjoying being at Shipdham School - but enjoys being at Letton even more!
Sarah has fled the nest for a while and is studying Sociology, Linguistics and Computer Studies at the University of Wales in Bangor - at least, she is trying to study, but apparently there's not much time left after involvement with the CU and local churches, and the general whirl of student life.
Simon is now working for KLM near Norwich Airport, on their Aircraft Engineers Training Scheme - although he was nearly put off flying altogether on a recent turbulent trip to Sweden.
Jonathan is in his first term teaching at a Comprehensive School in Thetford, battling with the challenge of educating reluctant pupils.
Gerald is enjoying his ministry training course, but understands "the real work starts in January" Meantime he is finding plenty to do in the day (and night) job at Letton.
June is kept even busier running around after the family, as well as carrying out her role as Letton's Housekeeper, Caterer, Shopkeeper etc etc. She is grateful for the good team that are supporting her, but as we look ahead to a full year 2000, it seems likely she will need even more back up.

Finally came the announcement in Letton News no.46 that they felt their term was coming to an end, and they would be handing on their roles to Richard and Rachel Kehoe.

Letton News No.46

June and Gerald on Letton's East Drive

Another year has flown by and the Letton story continues. Nothing seems to stand still for very long!

June and Gerald are moving on!

Last September we told you of many answers to prayer concerning our diverse staffing needs and we still continue to give thanks to God for the people he brought us, all skilled in just the right areas and all sure that The Lord brought them together. There is a great sense of joy and fulfilment in knowing you are where He wants you, doing what He wants you to do with the skills that He has given you and with a "family" of others that He has made you part of!

June and Gerald joined us in 1995 with a clear calling to The Lord's work here and soon found they had what must have seemed an insurmountable number of goals which they have steadily and faithfully worked toward. These included improvements in our financial and administrative stability, improved occupancy, upgraded facilities, a complete team of dedicated workers and many other issues, all for the express purpose of blessing God's people from whatever background.

We can see that, by and large, these goals have been met and June and Gerald now feel that their time here is coming to an end.

June and Gerald Rootham.

RESIDENT COUPLE PROFILE: BRIAN AND JANET ADAMS

Brian and Janet with the Carrolls.

Letton News no.31, Autumn 1998 (the "Mosaic Edition") announced how the Adams family first made contact with Letton before arriving for their ten month stay, starting from January 1999:

It started with a small ad in the Update Newsletter of CCI(UK), the organisation that keeps Christian Conferences up-to-date with news, views, resources and ideas. **Brian and Janet Adams** from Wellington in New Zealand were offering to help out at a Christian Centre on a voluntary basis for 10 months of 1998. We exchanged faxes and photgraphs; an outline programme was drawn up; with prayer, plans and decisions were made; and in January the Adams arrived. This was the general "mosaic design" ..... but from here on, the full picture developed as all the individuals involved made their individual contribution in all the different tasks and situations that followed.

In arranging an "exchange" such as this, there was a certain amount of risk involved on both sides, but it was the **Adams** who had to put their faith into action first. They had to let their home for a year, uproot their family, and set out into the unknown. On the other hand, one of their main impressions by the end was how much people at Letton have trusted them, and brought them fully into the work. They have enjoyed meeting and working with the wide variety of people involved with Letton - and they even maintain they enjoyed living in the Dower Flat, despite the noisy Carroll family on the floor above them!

Brian,
Janet.
Matt,
David
Jonathin
E Grant.

There has been lots of hard work, they admit, and occasional embarrassing moments (such as when Brian appeared, having been called out quite early in the morning by a group leader, with the comb still in his hair .....!) but our memories of them are very warm ... memories of Janet's "special touches" in the kitchen and of Brian's wit and wisdom, plus his unending enthusiasm for running go-kart sessions. And both **Matt** and David have made their own individual marks with their own friends and contacts.

But the mosaic picture for them is not completely finished, because their future is uncertain. One of their aims in coming to Letton was to test out their calling to "constant Christian hospitality", with a view to taking on a family property in New Zealand for this purpose ..... but the property is now not available. So we pray with them for God's guidance for what lies ahead - and we thank them very greatly for all they have contributed and achieved here at Letton.

After their return to New Zealand they reported back on progress in Letton News no.33, Autumn 1999:

NEWS FROM NEW ZEALAND

Greetings to our many friends linked with Letton! Hardly a day goes by without us mentioning something about our time there and the many groups that we got to know. We miss the Letton Lifestyle - those really busy weekends with constant people - the cooking and the go-karts!

Early in the year we received an offer to work at Totara Springs in Matamata - an amazing complex. At Parachute Christian Music Festival 15,000 go there camping out and using the full facilities. It is well known to us as we used to go there as a family when the boys were growing up - but we didn't feel that this was meant for us, and our prayers and conversations confirmed that we should wait.

We have looked at a number of other opportunities but each time we feel that we are to wait and be available for our children and elderly parents at the moment - and that there will be another "window of opportunity", as at Letton Hall. We have been asked if we would fill in for a couple in Nepal in the Missionary Hospital whilst they have a break but this will depend on Visas etc. So we are not sweating or worrying, and are enjoying our decision not to go back into the corporate business world. We have set up a home business together producing Business and Fashion cards which enables us to be flexible with time - and also builds up strong arm muscles as the process is a manual one!

We send our love to you, wishing you God's richest blessings at this time of the year. Whilst we are celebrating on the beaches with BBQ's and swimming, you will be having a white Christmas with roaring fires! We are looking forward to our first UK visitor, Simon Alexander from Mattishall and we would love to see others from the Letton family too!

With all our love - **Brian, Janet, Matthew and David Adams**

Their visit was a great success, remembered for Brian and Janet's boundless energy and enthusiasm, and for their warm-hearted love of people. Their visit also enabled both the Carrolls and the Roothams to have sabbatical breaks.

They were invited back for another equally successful four-month spell in the Spring of 2001.

RESIDENT COUPLE PROFILE:
BILL AND VAL CRUDGINGTON

Letton News No. 36 May 2003

Letton Hall Trust, Shipdham, Thetford Norfolk IP25 7SA   Tel 01362 820717

New Resident Couple

Bill and Valerie Crudgington are joining us this month and will be taking up residence in the Dower Flat as soon as we have remedied the freshly discovered dry rot in their bedroom! We thank God for providing them in His good time. June, Gerald and Stephen have soldiered on since autumn 2002, since Peter and Kay moved to Norwich and it would not be possible for them to go through the spring and summer without more resident team cover.

Bill and Valerie have recently returned from Jerusalem where they were involved in the management of Christ Church Guest House. They bring their skills and experience to Letton in their roles of assisting June and Gerald in the next phase of our ministry.

New Resident Couple

Bill and Valerie Crudgington are joining us this month and will be taking up residence in the Dover Flat as soon as we have remedied the freshly discovered dry rot in their bedroom! We thank God for providing them in His good time. June, Gerald and Stephen have soldiered on since autumn 2002, since Peter and Kay moved to Norwich and it would not be possible for them to go through the spring and summer without more resident team cover.

Bill and Valerie have recently returned from Jerusalem where they were involved in the management of Christ Church Guest House. They bring their skills and experience to Letton in their roles of assisting June and Gerald in the next phase of our ministry.

Bill and Val Crudgington, who live and work on site, are hoping that at some point next year we might let them retire which, whilst a blessing for them after their faithful ministry here, presents us with a significant challenge! Replacing a couple like Bill and Val who have served so faithfully and know Letton so well, is not going to be easy. Please make the need known and join us in praying for God to guide us clearly in making this important appointment.

Please contact Danny in the first instance if you would be interested in the position.

Email: daniel@lettonhall.org

N HALL   LN 52

Bill and Valerie Crudgington

RESIDENT COUPLE PROFILE:
RICHARD AND RACHEL KEHOE

Letton News - No.47

After 15 years Gerald and June Rootham are handing on management of Letton Hall to Richard and Rachel Kehoe

Double delight!

The trustees are delighted that a new era is about to begin with Richard and Rachel Kehoe at the helm and delighted with the healthy position June and Gerald have ably steered Letton to, sometimes through stormy and difficult waters, always with Jesus as their pilot!

When, last October, the Roothams felt the Lord calling them away from Letton to make way for fresh people to take the centre to a new level, we had to accept that it was indeed The Lord's timing and that He would not be calling June and Gerald elsewhere without providing us with His choice for the next couple, for the next stage of the Letton journey.

After much prayer and applications from over 25 candidates, the selection process was still not easy, as several candidates had such highly relevant experience.

But we can now rejoice that The Lord has brought the Kehoes to Letton. They hope to spend some time here before the Roothams leave on 27th April but may not be fully in-harness until early in May.

And the Roothams are happy to be around part-time in May as they start to move into their more formal leadership role at their church (All Saints, Mattishall).

A Warm Welcome to
Richard and Rachel Kehoe

Richard and Rachel believe that God has opened a door for them to serve Him here at Letton. They come to us after serving for 4 years as managers of Le Pas Opton, Spring Harvest's holiday campsite in France. In addition to managing and improving our family group facilities and accommodation, they have a desire to improve our activities facilities and create an environment where more children and young people, hopefully in school groups, can explore our faith and discover the Bible in creative ways, woven into a programme that actually complements the national curriculum.

Richard and Rachel Kehoe have also decided to step down from their role at Letton Hall, to move on to new things. Their enthusiasm and love for Letton was a catalyst for many developments and improvements in the last few years - and their contribution will be greatly missed. Their impact on the buildings, grounds and facilities has been considerable; but what they have contributed to the ambience, welcome and warmth of Letton Hall has been greater still — who will forget the amazing history tours, activities and events they organised? Please pray for them both as they seek God's direction for the future and take up new opportunities.

17

RESIDENT COUPLE PROFILE:
DANNY AND ALISON PRITCHARD

Letton News

Edition No.52   Winter 2013

Coming home to Letton Hall!

Although we are new to the team at Letton Hall, we are not strangers to Norfolk! Alison was born in Thetford and Danny's family relocated to Norfolk in 1973.

In December 1991 after several years serving the Lord as evangelists with Youth for Christ across East Anglia, we moved our young family from Norwich to Mayfield in East Sussex, where Danny took up a new post as Regional Co-ordinator for YFC. In the years that followed we became part-time leaders in our local church and eventually Danny was ordained as a Baptist Minister and we pastored Baptist churches in Battle and on the outskirts of Brighton.

In 2009 we joined the team at Ashburnham Christian Trust and became thoroughly immersed in a community and ministry providing retreat and conference facilities for God's people.

So, after more than 20 years away, we have come home – home to Norfolk and to our new home at Letton Hall.

We have known and loved Letton since the early days when Peter Carroll first opened the doors of the Hall to guests and we are so glad to be part of this special work.

Danny was Director for Ministry and led the overseas volunteer programme and Alison served in the bookings and reception department, involved with guest contact and customer liaison. We anticipated being at Ashburnham Place for some years, but unknown to us, God was using our short time there as a preparation for something else.

When we heard that the Trustees at Letton Hall were looking for new Centre Managers we were interested, as we had fond memories of many visits to Letton, some years ago – but it took a month for us to sense that perhaps God was asking us to consider the position.

Through prayer, meetings with the Trustees and our interview it was confirmed for us all that though unexpected, this turn of events was not untimely and very much in the purposes of God.

So, since 1st February, we have been finding our way around and learning the ropes, encouraged and supported by our excellent team. We are impressed by how much the ministry of Letton Hall blesses our guests.

We are looking forward to discerning God's priorities for this season as we together shape Letton's programmes and bring them into being. Feedback from friends and guests is assisting us as we consider which improvements and upgrades are necessary and appropriate for Letton Hall's future.

Do feel free to be a part of that. We would welcome your calls, emails or indeed your visits!

We very much look forward to meeting you in the coming months.

Danny & Alison Pritchard

Danny & Alison write...

LN 59 – November 2013

Danny & Alison Pritchard
The Dower Flat,
Letton Hall
November 2013

After nine months, including a busy summer programme, we are feeling quite settled in our roles at Letton Hall and feel greatly privileged to be serving the Lord here. We love our new home and our two West Highland Terriers, Molly and Lizzy, are thoroughly enjoying the freedom and fun of walks around the Letton woodland. All of our family have had the opportunity to visit and we are enjoying being closer to our parents who live just half an hour away in Thetford.

Life is never dull here and every day brings fresh experiences of God's blessings and provision along with new tests of faith and a steep learning curve! It has been a joy to meet many of the regular Letton visitors - often giving us the opportunity to renew old friendships - and also to welcome people here for the first time. We are so blessed to have an excellent team around us, who know more about the day-to-day running of Letton Hall than we do and have been very patient and kind while the managers are still wearing the 'L' plates. They are all very hard working and dedicated and motivated by a desire to give the best possible experience to our guests week by week. Although most of them are quite happy serving in the background, in this and future newsletters, we hope to introduce some of them to you, so that you can pray for them and perhaps recognise them when you visit!

As you read on, you will discover that this continues to be a season of change for us all and we greatly appreciate the love and prayers of our friends as we negotiate the challenges ahead.

Thank you so much for your interest, prayers and practical support. We are greatly encouraged by your fellowship with us in our work for the Lord.

Danny & Alison

LETTON HALL

18

FAMILY WEEK MEMORIES

There are many memories of family weeks that make each one special to those who were involved, be they 'guests' or 'team' - and one of the features of family weeks was the fact that divisions between visitors and staff quickly disappeared; we were all soon united as one 'family' as the week went on. Amidst all these memories it is difficult to pick out any without being aware of the many that were every bit as special that are being left out. However, here are two that I remember.

A CHRISTMAS TRANSFORMATION

One of our main aims in holding Christmas house parties was to be able to invite to them anyone who would otherwise be spending the holiday on their own, or at least not in a family atmosphere. There was naturally a lot of excitement over the four or five days they lasted and one of the features was the amount of mess created by a house full of children enjoying themselves - quite unbelievable at times!

One of my roles was to get up early each day and light the fire in the Library, to make it homely and cosy - and after I had done this to spend quite a while clearing up the mess from the night before and putting everything back in its place. One year, to my amazement, the house was absolutely clean and tidy when I came down on the first morning. Who had got up earlier than me and tidied it all up? On the second morning the same thing had happened, but nobody had mentioned anything, and by the time it happened for the third time my curiosity got the better of me and I asked around.

Eventually one young mother 'confessed.' It was her first time at Letton and her first time away with her child at Christmas - and she had left behind a really troubled family situation, and had no background of Christian faith. She was desperately unhappy and couldn't sleep at all through the night. The only way she could occupy her mind was to tidy up the house in the small hours of the morning without saying a word to anybody.

On the last morning I came into the Library - and a scene of devastation met me. It was just how it had been left the night before. What had happened to my secret helper? I became quite worried, until I heard the full story ... Several of the other mums had heard of her situation and spent hours chatting with her, telling her about the love of Jesus and using the Christmas story to explain what Jesus could mean to her. It was really Good News for her, she committed her life to Jesus - and slept like a log for the whole night!

I missed her help - but was so pleased she had at last been able to rest in the love of God.

A POIGNANT STORY

The designation on the back of a framed picture (see opposite and overleaf) hanging in a Letton bedroom tells a remarkable story, which started when Louise was staying at a Family Week and was told by a phone call from her doctor that the results of her tests were not good ...

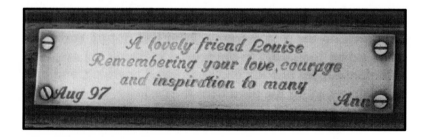

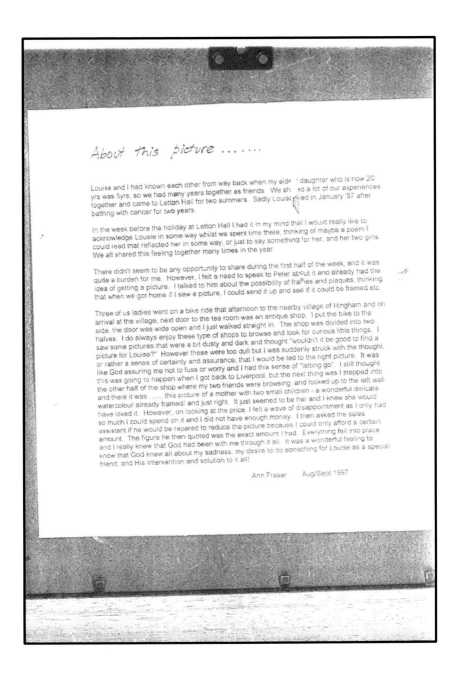

About this picture ....

Louise and I had known each other from way back when my elde[...] daughter who is now 20 yrs was 5yrs, so we had many years together as friends. We sh[...]ed a lot of our experiences together and came to Letton Hall for two summers. Sadly Louise died in January '97 after battling with cancer for two years.

In the week before the holiday at Letton Hall I had it in my mind that I would really like to acknowledge Lousie in some way whilst we spent time there, thinking of maybe a poem I could read that reflected her in some way, or just to say something for her, and her two girls. We all shared this feeling together many times in the year.

There didn't seem to be any opportunity to share during the first half of the week, and it was quite a burden for me. However, I felt a need to speak to Peter about it and already had the idea of getting a picture. I talked to him about the possibility of frames and plaques, thinking that when we got home if I saw a picture, I could send it up and see if it could be framed etc.

Three of us ladies went on a bike ride that afternoon to the nearby village of Hingham and on arrival at the village, next door to the tea room was an antique shop. I put the bike to the side, the door was wide open and I just walked straight in. The shop was divided into two halves. I do always enjoy these type of shops to browse and look for curious little things. I saw some pictures that were a bit dusty and dark and thought "wouldn't it be good to find a picture for Louise?" However these were too dull but I was suddenly struck with the thought, or rather a sense of certainty and assurance, that I would be led to the right picture. It was like God assuring me not to fuss or worry and I had this sense of "letting go". I still thought this was going to happen when I got back to Liverpool, but the next thing was I stepped into the other half of the shop where my two friends were browsing, and looked up to the left wall and there it was ...... this picture of a mother with two small children - a wonderful delicate watercolour already framed! and just right. It just seemed to be her and I knew she would have loved it. However, on looking at the price, I felt a wave of disappointment as I only had so much I could spend on it and I did not have enough money. I then asked the sales assistant if he would be repared to reduce the picture because I could only afford a certain amount. The figure he then quoted was the exact amount I had. Everything fell into place and I really knew that God had been with me through it all. It was a wonderful feeling to know that God knew all about my sadness, my desire to do something for Louise as a special friend, and His intervention and solution to it all!

Ann Fraser   Aug/Sept 1997

SPRING HOUSE PROJECT

AUTUMN 1992
Nº 22

Letton Hall, Shipdham, Norfolk

LETTON NEWS

PROJECTS REVIEW

Completed projects are a spur to our faith - but this year several are still in progress. A challenge to our faith!

* The SPRING HOUSE PROJECT, funded by **Tim and Sally Nicholson** and engineered by **Graham Arram** has been a major venture - and is still not yet finally completed. Work parties led by Graham and Tim started work in April, and with **Chris Eglington's** help, first built a road to the spring (only half a dozen words on paper, but several weeks of mud and rain and several hundred tons of earthmoving, in practice!) Then the Spring house itself was ringed with sacks of reinforced concrete lowered into a trench, the tiling taken off and the roof jacked up. The pool then was surrounded by interlocking metal piling driven into the sand and clay and specially-cast concrete edging put into place. New brick pillars were built to support the roof - and with bated breath, the roof lowered onto them. At the time of writing, there are still a few more pillars to be built and roof tiling and walls to be replaced - but our water supply is now secure! The roll of honour for this venture included the regular **Letton** team, as well as the **Arram, Nicholson and Lodge** families, **Neil and Karen Pitcher** with young **Katie,** Karen's parents **Roy and Penny Schroder**.... all were vital for mini-digger driving, bricklaying, cooking and various other roles. Other invaluable helpers included **Jonathan Thurley, Glen Jones, Michael Freed, Paddy McDermot, Bill Platt, Terry Martin, Lyn Dobson and Daniel, Abigail Weeks** and probably many others who got their wellies wet but didn't leave their footprints for the record!

LETTON NEWS

NUMBER 27
AUTUMN 1995

DRINKING WATER

Our regular programme of water testing is still producing good results, but we have
continued to make improvements to the Ultra-Violet Water treatment system, to cover
all eventualities (i.e. power failure), and also to keep pace with the ever-tightening
requirements of the Environmental Health Department.

For the future, they would like to see the water tower removed from the supply system,
in case it harbours contamination. Otherwise, to clean it thoroughly internally, we
require a regular contract with a frogman/steeplejack with hot high-pressure jet
equipment - so if you know of one please let us know!

The best option at the moment seems to be to install low level storage tanks near the
foot of the water tower, and pump to the taps and tanks on demand. One good source of
tanks seems to be (don't laugh) a bank of giant 300 gallon orange squash bottles
(we are, after all, near the nation's squash capital, Robinsons of Norwich!).
However, alternative schemes are being costed ...

On the subject of Environmental Health etc, the local Authority in their dealings with
us, have recently amalgamated Safety at Work and Fire Safety under this heading, and
have sent a letter to all Trustees outlining work that still needs to be done, and
asking for a timescale. Obviously, we are committed to doing this, but to produce an
accelerated timetable and make a firm commitment to it, requires a very hard look at
our finances.

On the other side of the coin, we are hoping that the nearly-free-to-run hydraulic
rams will soon be operating - see page ....

WATER WORKS

Over the years many people have looked at the
hydraulic rams down at the spring, have heard how
they are designed to pump up water to the house
with no apparent power source other than the stream
running past, have realised the potential, but also
been daunted by the problems ..... and so have gone
away with a polite "oh, yes ...."

A BLAKE
HYDRAM

Not so, **Richard Simpson and Charlie Woods** (with
Chris and family as back up team). Richard
discovered, for instance, that the hydram
manufacturers were still in business, and could
confirm that two model 7x units were purchased on 11
September 1919, with serial numbers 13078 & 13080,
- and that spares were still available off the
shelf! It was tempting to ask if they were still
under guarantee, but it was felt only fair to do
some investigating work first (!) and accordingly
Richard and Charlie got down to it.

One of the rams pulsed back into life quite quickly but didn't deliver water to it's
design specification, with enough pressure to reach the top of the water tower. A
worn drive pipe was suspected, so this was investigated (with recording video camera
sent down inside the pipe - a technique that would surely have amazed the builders in
1919) and evidence of earlier repairs uncovered.

At the time of writing repairs have been completed, and one of the hydrams is
undergoing pumping trials. This project is coming at a particularly important stage,
as our water supply generally is under consideration, and the rams could play a really
vital role for the future. Thank you, Richard, Charlie and family, for all your
skill, time and effort and financial help!

PURCHASE APPEAL PROGRESS: 1

Letton News No 41 Summer 2006

Thank you for your continued interest and support. We are sending this interim Newsletter to keep you informed of current events and especially to update you about progress and current thoughts on the Letton Purchase Appeal.

The Current Position

The agreed discount price is	£960,000
To date, the amount donated is	£160,000
We have a loan facility of	£450,000
The shortfall, with 5 months to go, is therefore	£350,000

Please pray for Vic Winchcombe, our newly appointed fundraiser. Vic is currently contacting Trusts and other organisations. He asks that we pray for God to lead him to the right doors. It is refreshing to find a professional who seeks our prayers, and who acknowledges that he can do nothing without God.

Psalm 108 says"...for the help of man is **worthless. With God we shall gain the victory"**

Our Current thoughts

We have to face the possibility that the full amount may not be raised in time. We pray often about this and here are our current thoughts:

We still believe that The Lord told us to ask Him for the property, to establish the work of the trust for the future. But we do not claim to have had a promise from The Lord to give us £960k by 31 December 2006.

If The Lord does not give us the money by the deadline, it's Ok with us! But we cannot wash our hands of the responsibility to try every door.

If He chooses not to give us the money at all, that's also OK with us. But he *has* given £160k!

The Possibilities

By October we need to have decided:

1) Should we proceed with the purchase and somehow borrow the shortfall?
2) Should we try to extend the purchase option, probably at a higher price?
3) Should we take the shortfall as The Lord's guidance not to proceed?

We are waiting upon God and ask you all to pray please. His will is all we seek!

One persistent theme has been that the small amounts given in love by God's people are vital. We felt this from the start, hence the 20:20 Vision, but it has also been confirmed by several guests and supporters.

Option (1) would mean that the purchase appeal is ongoing and gives Vic more time to approach grant-making trusts. Any additional borrowing can only be justified by an increase in regular donations to fund the extra interest. We could consider increasing fees charged to visiting groups to steadily replace gifts as time goes on.

Option (2) would also mean that the purchase appeal would carry on. It is, however, entirely dependent upon Peter Carroll being willing to extend the option and the idea of a price increase does not have instant appeal!

Option (3) is always a possibility(!) But we will not simply take the path of least resistance. We will seek God's will.

Of course, these 3 options only apply if the funds do not arrive. We know of several groups and individuals still considering what to give.
So - please pray that the appeal succeeds !!

John Currey
On behalf of the Trustees and Team

Other News

Schools Programme Leaflet
Please pass it on to a teacher you know. Letton is a great venue for school residential trips.

Diary Dates
Bible Focus - 13th -16th November 2006
Our guest speaker is **Rev Philip Hacking**. Book now and please invite your friends.
Spring Retreat 8th - 11th May 2007
Following the 2006 series "Bible Mountains", Phil and Gwyn plan to lead a series on **Bible Valleys!** You can book now - but leaflets will follow later!

The work is flourishing
Read on and see what's been happening since Christmas! There's new plumbing and paint, new people, new prospects, new possibilities ...

PURCHASE APPEAL PROGRESS: 2

A message from John & The Trustees

The last 2 years were a roller-coaster ride! In recent Newsletters I've tried to keep you up to date about our thoughts, prayers and where we were with God's guidance.

The £260,000 target was achieved just before Christmas and we were about 75% of the way there on newly-promised ongoing donations to fund the £700,000 mortgage. After much prayer and a great meeting with our bank manager, the loan was agreed, subject to a valuation survey. This was also completed just before Christmas and the loan was made unconditional. What could we do? Within a few days of the deadline, God had given us what we asked for. We simply had to make the step of faith - not blind faith - 20:20 faith - confident that it was a step of obedience too. Since then, at a team prayer meeting, we read Haggai Ch 2. Some phrases which stood out as an encouragement were:

"The silver is mine and the Gold is mine...
..and in this place I will grant peace says the Lord of Hosts."

And then we sang a song which was completely new to me.

"All I have and all I am is yours;
There's nothing that I have on earth that doesn't come from you
I lay aside my pride and worldly worth;
To serve you is the greatest thing
That I could ever do....
...For unless You build this house,
I am building it in vain.
Unless the work is Yours,
There is nothing to be gained..."

Again, the words spoke volumes and we took them very much to heart. May we always be mindful of our responsibilities and thankful for the privilege of serving God in this way.

John Currey

LETTON NEWS: JUBILEE EDITION

LETTON News
50th Edition Spring 2012

A Victorian Christmas comes to Letton...

2012— The Year of the Diamond Jubilee, the Olympics, and our 50th Newsletter!

Welcome to our 50th edition. You might be somewhat surprised by the above photo, but this epitomises a big answer to prayer!

Letton Hall has been, for 33 years, a home where people have had an opportunity to meet with God. One of our deepest desires is to connect with and welcome in people from the local community. At the end of 2011, we did just that.

Resulting from a conversation with a guest at our recent Creative Writing week, we decided to hold an open day in the guise of 'A Victorian

Christmas'. The team planned and plotted a day of fun and (Victorian) frolic for anyone who might want to come.

Preparations were fun, intense and all inclusive, and the result... well, you can see from the photos! It was a fun-packed day with the whole team dressed in period costume and I'm delighted to report that we had over 250 visitors... many of whom had never been here before. One lady commented "I've driven past for over 15 years and never known what it was!".

God blessed us tremendously by bringing in far more people than we could have hoped for.

New Events for 2012!

See inside for details on the events we'll be running this year.

Be sure to sign up soon and bring your friends!

Not to be missed!

LETTON HALL

Only 15 minutes after the opening time, the place was already buzzing with activity—from those who were simply curious to others who dressed up in Victorian costume for the occasion!

Letton Hall staff took their characters from the 1851 census of those who lived and worked here. Guests were given a candlelit tour around four new rooms set up to show how life 'below stairs' used to be. They were even invited to have a go at churning butter, preparing the wine and 'mangling' in the laundry!

For others, the Victorian games were the big attraction— offering a chance to win sweets on Tin Can Alley, hoopla and shove ha'penny (and the slightly less authentic Go Karting!). There was also Ye Olde Shoppe for the sweet-tooth, selling old fashioned sweets by the quarter.

Meanwhile, upstairs, the Victorian and Christmas themed activities continued. Visitors were able to make traditional gifts, from cornucopias full of sweets, to Christmas crackers, découpage gift boxes, hampers, traditional mincemeat, sugar mice, peppermint creams and lavender sugar.

As so many people stayed for hours (and indeed all day!) we ended with a large crowd for our finale. Packed into the library with mulled wine and mince-pies all around, we enjoyed traditional carols and readings from the gospels about the birth of Jesus.

Our many thanks to everyone who came, especially those who volunteered to make it a very memorable day, and to Jeff and Rosemary Nicholls for their donation of so many Victorian treasures.

An interview with

Peter Carroll

For our 50th newsletter, we wanted to ask where did it all began....

VERY EARLY DAYS AT LETTON

The Carroll's arrived on 1 December 1979 with a clear sense of the Lord's direct guidance leading up to that moment. Looking at newsletter No 1 gives an idea of what it was like....

We discovered it was really quite large having counted 88 rooms; but it was also in need of urgent work including tackling dry rot and roof maintenance.

Work Parties came from far and wide to hack-off decayed plaster, remove rubble and rotten wood, have giant bonfires of rubbish – and make a start on redecorating.

Fergie the tractor arrived on Christmas Day, gift-wrapped with ribbon, to help with the outside work – and one group remembers starting to convert Dolphin Court from horses' living quarters into guest accommodation, including removing tons of horse 'leftovers'!

The first prayer letter canvassed support for all this, but also gave thanks that one brave group had booked to come in May 1980 for a holiday rather than hard labour.

Praise the Lord that people are still coming!

THE CHRISTIAN STORY OF LETTON

Over the years many people have experienced the Lord working and speaking through time spent at Letton. These encounters have often been helpful, sometimes life-changing...

I am intending to gather together in a book memories and stories, for further challenge and encouragement.

My role will be partly as narrator – since I have seen much of the Lord's work at Letton myself – but also as editor of contributions from others. These can be in your own words, or I can spend time (with pen and notebook at hand) listening to your stories.

So... if you have memories of miracles, moments of illumination, encouragements or excitements, testing times or times of thanksgiving, guidance, or just any personal experiences that you think people might like to know about – then please let me know!

Peter Carroll

peterjcarroll2000@yahoo.co.uk

You can buy a copy of Peter's new book 'The Lives and Loves of Letton Hall' by calling us on 01362 820717 or using the order form on our website at www.lettonhall.org

From the past to the future...
Richard & Rachel

Well that was Christmas, and a wonderful experience too. However, the team are now planning future events, so keep an eye on the website, and be assured - there will be plenty more costumes!

Our joy is to always welcome new people to Letton and the website is an integral part of increasing our presence in the minds of organisers, and to let them know what we offer. Our increased programme of events and activities will hopefully attract new guests and encourage our current friends to return.

An Unusual Appeal!

Does anyone know how we can track down a Bedouin tent? Rachel would like to include a Bible-times experience for School children who come to Letton and a genuine Bedouin tent would be perfect for old testament activities.

Thank you!

We are continuing to make improvements (finances permitting) to facilitate more guests. We are developing plans to better accommodate caravans and tents so that people can enjoy the pleasure of the grounds at Letton, without having to use our regular facilities. Thanks to customer feedback forms, we are also aware of other areas that we would enhance the guest experience, and we will continue to strive to improve matters. Perhaps you would like to get involved? Read on...

We hope you've discovered our new website, which took to the net last October. If you haven't take a look!

It now provides much for information for guests and promotes some new events and activities that we will be offering in 2012.

We have already been finding more enquiries coming through as a result of our new site!

Please take a look at: www.lettonhall.org

Also, if you are a social networker— find us on Facebook and Twitter!

Volunteers take on a
3 day challenge

It's great to be fully booked almost every weekend at Letton Hall and we praise God for this. However, it does make those big tasks a little daunting when we know that they must be started and completed in a few days!

In early February, we were blessed by a team of enthusiastic volunteers (known to Richard and Rachel from their time in France) with the job of transforming the drawing room and construct some much needed fencing.

Thank you to all the 'Vollies' who worked so hard to make it happen, especially the hardy men who braved the freezing cold temperatures outside!

If you would like to volunteer with us, come and have a coffee and chat about your skills and gifts, and what you would like to get involved in. For example, we would really appreciate an accountant giving just 1 day a fortnight to help us in the finance department. Thank you!

A word from the

Trustees

We've enjoyed watching Richard and Rachel settle into their management role, here at Letton. There have been some tough times and some real challenges.

Within weeks of their arrival, the water tower was condemned and the Fire Officer served a seriously long list of urgent upgrades required to the fire systems, fire doors etc.

Also, HM Revenue and Customs have suddenly made us charge VAT on all of our charges to groups. For the past 19 years we have, at their instigation, been partially exempt and this reversal of their position has forced us to increase our prices at a time when many guests are really feeling the pinch.

Despite these and many other challenges, the work flourishes. The team has bonded so well and I sense really joyful service, anticipation, achievement, encouragement and loving Christian fellowship as everyone supports each other and works so hard!

The visions for school ministry, local witness and niche events are gathering momentum. So, the list of prayer and praise is the same:

Protection, Provision, Guidance.

Please join us in prayer and give thanks with grateful hearts to our Heavenly Father.

From John Currey, on behalf of the Trustees

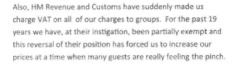

Chris Reyner, one of our long term supporters, died this January. She was a person who looked forward to heaven with an amazing sense of joy and anticipation. She will be missed, but we rejoice with her that she is with her Lord. We were also blessed to hold her funeral reception here, a place she had loved to be with her family.

Please join us in prayer for:

♦ Although we are booked up almost every weekend, we have found that the groups are smaller than they have been. This is disappointing for the group leaders and for us as we generate less income. Please pray that churches find ways to subsidise more people to come. Please also pray for us as we try other ways to cover costs.

♦ Pray that people will continue to draw nearer Jesus when they come to stay at Letton Hall.

♦ Pray for the team as they seek God for guidance for the vision for Letton. As we step forward with new events, we want to stay sensitive to the leading of the Holy Spirit, especially when it's easy to be distracted by day to day concerns!

♦ Pray for unity for the team at work and at home.

♦ Pray that we may be a bigger part of what God is doing nationally. Pray that we might be responsive, flexible, courageous and servant-hearted as we work in God's kingdom.

Brand New Events in 2012
Letton Events 2012

The Sole Houseparty

A brand new event at Letton Hall, aiming to provide 'the Great Escape' for single Christians between 25 and 40 years.

The week will consist of a fun-filled action-packed three night retreat with times of devotions and worship. See our website for more details.

Spring Break

This year, we will be welcoming Chick and Margaret Yuill as our speakers for Spring Break, from 8th -11th May 2012.

Chick works with churches to promote and facilitate the concept of Whole Life Discipleship. Do join us for this annual get together as we are challenged by God's word, enjoy old and new friendships, eat great food and enjoy all that Letton has to offer.

Creative Writing Week

We're delighted to be having Nick and Claire Page back again for another week of tuition, insight and imagination! Get away from it all and let your creative juices flow in the company of other like-minded writers (or those who would like to write!). If you're local, don't miss Nick's fascinating evening talks, open to anyone.

Family Week

Family week is aimed at single parent families. Come and enjoy a Letton summer holiday, brimming with adventure and fun activities, including go karting, archery, crafts, beach trips, games and campfires. A holiday of discovery, trying new things and just to enjoy being together... and guess what... no washing up! Just come!

Autumn Bible Focus

'Come Holy Spirit' with Stephen Mawditt. Three simple words that can bring transformation. How can we become more confident and assured in ministering in the power of the Holy Spirit?

Jesus declared 'The Kingdom of God is near'. His teaching amazed; His character astounded; His miracles astonished. We are called to be followers of Jesus. The same anointing available to Jesus is available to us, in all of this the role of the Holy Spirit is essential.

As we explore the ministry of the Counsellor promised by Jesus, expect to experience the Father's love. Join us!

We have several Christmas events in the pipeline, but you'll just have to wait until our Summer newsletter to find out what!

Guests make the most of the snow and construct a very impressive igloo in the walled garden!

£2 Coin Challenge—Are you up for it?!

We're so grateful for the blessings of bookings this year and for the way this has enabled us to make some big improvements to the standard of what we offer. We have been able to replace carpets, improve furnishings, paint rooms and upgrade some facilities.

However, in amongst the great feedback we get from our guests, is the age old complaint about water pressure in the showers. Due to the nature of the building, this is not an easy problem to solve.

Therefore, we would like to launch a new fundraising appeal!

We would like to challenge you to collect any £2 coins that you get given as change in the supermarket. It doesn't happen that often, but if it does, how about saving it and giving it to us in *The Great Shower Power Fundraiser!*

It's just for fun!

Thanks for all your support!

Love from the Letton Hall Team.

(seen here on a belated Christmas do with staff volunteers and trustees)

LETTON HALL

Letton Hall, Shipdham, Norfolk, IP25 7SA

01362 820717   ~   info@lettonhall.org

www.lettonhall.org   ~   Reg. Charity No: 279817

Lightning Source UK Ltd.
Milton Keynes UK
UKOW02f2030220115

244957UK00002B/2/P